THE DELICATESSEN COOKBOOK

The Delicatessen Cookbook
SUZANNE BEEDELL

PELHAM BOOKS

First published in Great Britain by
Pelham Books Ltd
52 Bedford Square
London WC1B 3EF
1973

© 1973 by Suzanne Beedell

All Rights Reserved. No part of this publication may be reproduced, stored in a retrieval system, or transmitted, in any form or by any means, electronic, mechanical, photocopying, recording or otherwise, without the prior permission of the Copyright owner

ISBN 0 7207 0703 X

Set and printed in Great Britain by
Northumberland Press Limited, Gateshead,
and bound by Dorstel Press, Harlow

CONTENTS

	WEIGHTS, MEASURES AND ABBREVIATIONS	9
	INTRODUCTION	11
1	Soups and Soup Additions	15
2	Fish and Shellfish	22
3	Meat, Sausages, Game and Poultry, and Pâté	37
4	Vegetables	51
5	Fruit	85
6	Bread, Crispbreads, Cereals and Flours	98
7	Rice and Rice Dishes	108
8	Pasta and Popcorn	112
9	Pulses	117
10	Cheese and Other Milk Products	123
11	Nuts and Seeds	131
12	Sauces, Batters, Mayonnaise, Dressings, Syrups and Oils	138
13	Herbs and Seasonings	151
	ACKNOWLEDGEMENTS	166
	INDEX	167

Ten illustrations are between pages 80 and 81

WEIGHTS AND MEASURES CONVERSION TABLES

Oven Temperature Equivalents

DEGREES FAHRENHEIT	DEGREES CENTIGRADE	GAS MARK	
225	107	¼	Very cool oven
250	121	½	Very cool oven
275	135	1	Cool oven
300	149	2	Cool oven
325	163	3	Warm oven
350	177	4	Moderate oven
375	191	5	Fairly hot oven
400	204	6	Hot oven
425	218	7	Hot oven
450	232	8	Very hot oven
475	246	9	Very hot oven

Weight Equivalents

AVOIRDUPOIS	METRIC
1 ounce	= 28·35 grammes
1 lb	= 453·6 grammes
2·3 lb	= 1 kilogram

Liquid Measurements

¼ pint	=	1½ decilitres
½ pint	=	¼ litre
scant 1 pint	=	½ litre
1¾ pints	=	1 litre
1 gallon	=	4·5 litres

Easy Liquid Measures

½ pint	=	20 fluid oz	=	32 tablespoons
1 pint	=	10 fluid oz	=	16 tablespoons

¼ pint	=	5 fluid oz	=	8 tablespoons
1/8th pint	=	2½ fluid oz	=	4 tablespoons
1/16th pint	=	1¼ fluid oz	=	2 tablespoons

American Measures

16 fluid oz = 1 American pint
8 fluid oz = 1 American standard cup
·50 fluid oz = 1 American tablespoon (very slightly smaller than British)
·16 fluid oz = 1 American teaspoon

Abbreviations

tbspn = tablespoonful
dssrtspn = dessertspoonful
tspn = teaspoonful

Introduction

I noticed that my greengrocer was stocking more and more unusual fruits and vegetables; unusual, that is, for a small seaside town on the Kent coast. I asked him how much of these things he sold, and he replied that he would sell a lot more if people had any idea how to cook them. From this remark came the idea for this book. There are so many cookery books in print that one can find recipes for anything under the sun somewhere. But because ingredients and recipes are regional, so are cookery books, and you need many books to find recipes for all the ingredients which are now on sale in grocers' shops and general delicatessens throughout this country.

Only ten years ago even a general delicatessen was rare in a small town. The best grocers sold a few unusual odds and ends; but only in the cities, and often only in London could one find the hundreds of things now sold in every town of any size at all. Because the general delicatessen shop and the good greengrocers' shop now sell fruit, vegetables, pasta, cheese, bread, cooked meats, spices and herbs from all over the world I thought it might be a good idea to bring together in one book recipes and suggestions for using those things which are still strange to many British cooks.

Granted many foods are still expensive here, but one must remember that in their countries of origin they are usually cheap and plentiful and part of everyday food, although they are luxuries to us. Where they grow, avocado pears are literally two a penny! Aubergines and courgettes are common vegetables to the Mediterranean housewife. The Indian housewife knows exactly which spices she must mix to make differing curry powders, and how to cook the variety of spiced dishes she is very familiar with. Because these things are used everyday elsewhere, recipes for cooking them are everyday recipes, easy to make and not requiring vast experience or training.

This book should also help the housewife who has tried to

use unfamiliar ingredients but who hasn't been able to find information about them or a recipe, so has resorted to cookery methods adequate for familiar things, and has produced a disaster of a dish which has put her off anything and everything different for life.

It can be argued that our British fruit, vegetables and meat are so good, so perfectly flavoured that they need little additional flavouring or fancy cooking, and that there is nothing better than 'good plain English food'. Well, that is absolutely true when the food is well cooked, but however fine the roast beef or the steak, the green peas or the buttered parsnips, the strawberries and cream or the apple pie, it is nice to have a change sometimes. And unfortunately, second-rate English cooking is dreadful; wasteful, and with a pitifully limited range, unimaginative, and tasteless.

Many of the thousands of us who have been abroad have perhaps picked up a taste for some foreign dishes and fruits, and have regrets at not being able to get them here outside expensive foreign restaurants. Now that we can get the ingredients from our local greengrocers and delicatessens, all that remains is to know how to cook and serve them.

You will not find here recipes for cooking standard English dishes, and I am assuming that you are familiar with basic cookery methods—boiling, grilling marinating, etc. Herbs and spices have been listed with short details because they are vital ingredients of so many dishes, and except for a few have long been neglected in English cookery; and they can all be bought from delicatessens.

Recipes have been included where they seem to fit, but there is inevitably some cross referencing. All the main recipes for an ingredient are given under its own specific heading, but a check with the Index may well lead you to other uses in combination with other ingredients. Check herbs and spices as they come up in recipes with the details in Section 13.

The French writer, Anthelme Brillat-Savarin said that 'The discovery of a new dish does more for the happiness of mankind than the discovery of a star'.* Undoubtedly, but both exercises are just about as difficult! Good cookery, any cookery,

---

* *Philosopher in the Kitchen*, 1825.

is the art of creating endless variations on basic themes which subdivide again and again. There are thousands of ingredients, and millions of cooks. So the permutations are astronomical, yet there can be nothing absolutely new. By adding more or less of this or that ingredient one can produce differing dishes; but are they really new? Boil oatmeal in water and you have porridge. Season that porridge with salt and you have something a little different. Serve it with cream and white sugar, or cream and brown sugar, or golden syrup, or cook the oatmeal in milk, not in water—all are different.

However simple or complex the dish the variations can be infinite or infinitesimal, so it follows that there is a dilemma for the cookery writer. Each recipe should be written down in exact terms, so much of this and so much of that, yet the writer knows that the permutations, even within the framework of one recipe, are again endless. Slight variations in quality alter taste. New fresh chilli powder, for instance, is much hotter than stale chilli powder, and there is no exact degree of hotness which can be declared on the tin to help the cook. So it must eventually be a matter of tasting and smelling. Recipes and pictures are guides, ideas and suggestions, not orders, and are capable of adaption by different cooks for varying tastes, and no cook should follow them slavishly.

I own a splendid Edwardian cookery book, full of marvellous recipes, most of which are extremely complicated. Almost every page carries an engraved illustration of a dish which would take hours to set up, let alone cook. Yet surprisingly, almost every recipe in the book is capable of simplification without losing any of its excellence, especially using modern prepared ingredients; and can be well presented at table without being fancied up at all like those engravings. For the housewife who does not nowadays employ a cook and various housemaids, the days of complex cookery are gone; she has neither the time nor the inclination to follow the dictates of my Edwardian book. She is instead overwhelmed by beautiful photographs of beautiful food, in lush cookery books. However good the recipes are (and most of them *are* good), she probably never produces anything which looks quite like those lovely photographs. She doesn't know, perhaps, that colour photography done in a studio really does make everything look twice as large as life and twice as natural—and heaven help us when they find a way to impregnate pages with the appropriate smells!

It is your skill and flair as a cook, your experience in different cooking techniques, plus your sensual judgement which will make these recipes into good meals.

Which brings up another point. Food which pleases you may revolt someone else. Their senses may reject what you enjoy, their conditioning make it impossible for them to eat what you relish. So I have another problem: to choose recipes which will generally fulfill, with personal adjustments, your taste requirements; but there is a wide range here and I hope I have not left anything vital out. Use these recipes to widen your repertoire by experimentation and to gain experience of new foods. None of the recipes is difficult.

Of course there are many hundreds of other ingredients sold by delicatessen not included herein. Most of these have adequate instructions on their packets or can only be used in obvious and limited ways, or are ingredients whose use is adequately covered in standard cookery books.

Anyway, I hope that some of the ideas and suggestions in this book will match up with your tastes and abilities and will lure you, gastronomically, ever onward.

SECTION ONE

Soups and Soup Additions

More recipes for making soup from specific ingredients can be found under their separate headings: Avocado soup, for instance, being located under 'Avocado' in the fruit section. Look also under 'Soup' in the Index.

With the soups sold in tins and packets at delicatessens you should follow the instructions given. Yet many of these soups can be vastly improved upon, or made more substantial by the judicious addition of wine, sherry, stock, noodles, dumplings, croûtons, grated cheese (usually Parmesan), chopped herbs, spicy seasonings, cream, cream cheese, egg, rice, boiling sausage, bacon and ham.

Tins and packets should have the ingredients they contain listed upon them, so to make more of them try to use identical additions. For instance a soup claiming to have red wine in it, will probably only contain a very small amount and more red wine added when heating it up can but improve it!

Croûtons go with any and every soup (see page 16).

ALCOHOL

Add alcohol—wine, cognac, sherry, Marsala or whatever—to soup just before it is served, and do not boil it once it has been added. How much to add can only be judged by taste; a dessertspoonful per serving is usually plenty.

CLEAR SOUPS

Consommes and broths are often much improved by a dash of sherry. Broths and clear soups will take all kinds of noodles, spatzle (see page 115) dumplings (see page 104), gnocchi or rice. These should be added to the soup as it is heating and allowed to cook until tender but not mushy, which usually takes only about five minutes. Rice should be precooked as it does take longer and will absorb too much soup so that you end up with soup flavoured rice, not garnished soup. Never overdo things when adding pasta to soup; remember that it will swell and absorb much liquid. A tablespoonful per serving is more than enough of most pastas.

To thicken consommé or broth and make it more nourishing, add to it one egg yolk well beaten with a tablespoonful of cream, per tin. Beat the egg first, add a little hot soup and stir it well, add the cream, and stir again.

Let the soup drop below boiling point and add the egg and cream mixture, stirring all the time till the soup thickens, but take great care not to let it boil or to stop stirring, or it will curdle.

Chopped parsley or chopped chives go especially well with clear soups.

CREAM SOUPS

Add dollops of salted whipped cream, Ayrshire cream cheese or sour cream to enrich cream soups. Add spices and chopped herbs to lift and bring out flavour, and sherry to liven it up, although this can be a little dominant and cover up delicate creamy flavours.

THICK SOUPS

Purée soup made with peas, beans, lentils, etc., will take slices of cooked boiling sausage, frankfurters, etc., pieces of crisped bacon, or ham, or sliced hard-boiled eggs, grated cheese, sour cream or salted whipped cream or cream cheese.

CROÛTONS FOR SOUP

Bread	Paprika
Butter	Cheese
Olive Oil	Herbs
Salt	

Dice the bread and saute it in a half-and-half mixture of very hot oil and butter till evenly brown and crisp. Drain, and serve so hot that the croûtons splutter in the soup.

To make cheese and herb croûtons, spread slices of bread

with butter, dice them, and cook in a medium oven until brown. Put salt, pepper, ground Parmesan and such herbs as you like into a saucepan; add the croûtons and shake with the lid on until they are thoroughly coated.

MIXED SOUPS

Splendid rich soups can be made by mixing together the contents of various tins; this is one good way to use the better quality tinned soups available from delicatessens. Here are two examples:

Lobster Supreme

1 tin cream of asparagus soup	1 small carton double cream
1 tin cream of mushroom soup	4 tbspn dry sherry
1 small tin of lobster meat	Salt and pepper to taste

Blend the two tins of soup and heat without boiling, add the lobster meat without breaking it up into shreds. Just before serving, gently stir in the sherry, adjust the seasoning, and swirl the cream into the soup in its tureen.

Crab meat can be substituted for the lobster, but does tend to break into shreds. Prawns, shrimps or scampi, also go well in this soup, but you will have to change its name accordingly. Some fish is saltier than others, so be very careful that you do not oversalt this soup.

Tomato Corn Soup

2 tins cream of tomato soup	2 tbspn dry sherry
1 small tin cream sweet corn	Salt and pepper
2 whole skinned tomatoes	¼ pint top of the milk

Put together, in the pot in which you will bring the soup to the table, the soup, sweet corn and top of the milk. Cut the tomatoes into halves and float them in the soup. Put the uncovered dish in the oven at 325 deg (Gas 3) and cook until the contents have just reached boiling point. Remove from the oven, correct the seasoning, add the sherry and serve immediately.

VEGETABLE GARNISH

Tinned soups are much improved by the addition of the appropriate fresh vegetables as a garnish:

Casseroled Cream of Tomato Soup

2 tins cream of tomato soup	Basil
3 firm whole tomatoes, skinned	Salt and black pepper
Cream	Stock

Empty the tins of soup into a casserole or 'marmite' with a handle and dilute with just a little stock. With the lid on, or covered with baking foil, bring the soup to the boil. Halve the tomatoes and float them in the soup, sprinkle in a little crushed dried basil, and season to taste. Allow to cook in a medium oven for 15 minutes with the lid on, and 5 minutes with it off. Swirl in a good dollop of thick cream and bring it to the table in the pot in which it was cooked.

Asparagus, mushroom, celery and other vegetable soups can be tarted up in the same way, but omit the basil.

SOUP ADDITIONS

Soup	*Additions*
Artichoke	Cream Chervil
Asparagus	Diced hard-boiled egg
Beetroot or Bortsch	Sour cream Grated cucumber Cooked boiling sausage Red wine
Birds Nest	Chicken stock Shredded ham and pork and/ or chicken
Bisques	Thick cream Cayenne pepper Celery seed, mustard seed Dry cabbage

Soup	Additions
Cabbage	Sour cream, salted whipped cream Ayrshire cream cheese Caraway seed, fennel seed
Cauliflower	Grated cheese
Celery	Grated nutmeg Marjoram Grated cheese
Chicken (broth)	Coriander, allspice, cloves, curry powder Celery seed, mustard seed Bay, rosemary, thyme Grated cheese Thinly sliced cucumber or lemon Noodles, gnocchi, spatzle (see page 115), vermicelli, matzo dumplings (see page 104)
Chicken (cream of)	Celery seed Marjoram, sage, chives
Cock-a-leekie	Cream
Consommé (hot)	Sour cream Allspice, curry powder Sherry, Madeira
Consommé Madrilène (cold)	Sour cream Red caviare Diced avocado Orange juice and thin orange slices
Fish, Chowder, Bouillabaisse	Cayenne pepper, allspice, Bay, rosemary, parsley, thyme, lemon
Fruit	Anise, cinnamon Dill

Soup	Additions
Game	Juniper berries, cloves Port, sherry
Gazpacho (cold)	Diced cucumber, peppers
Kangaroo Tail	Sherry
Lentil	Swirl of olive oil Oregano, mint Black pepper Cooked boiling sausage, bacon or ham
Minestrone	Pesto sauce (see page 146) to turn it into 'Pistou' soup Basil, oregano Grated Parmesan cheese Boiling sausage, ham or salami pieces
Mulligatawny	Hot cream Lemon juice
Mushroom	Whipped cream, Ayrshire cream cheese Parsley, chives, tarragon Dry sherry, Marsala
Onion	Grated cheese on toasted French bread, browned in the oven Cloves, marjoram, nutmeg Cognac
Oxtail	Lemon juice Sherry, Marsala
Pea and Bean	Cream Chilli powder, coriander, nutmeg, curry powder, paprika Tarragon, oregano, basil, mint Cooked boiling sausage, bacon, ham

Soup	Additions
Potato	Cream, Ayrshire cream cheese Allspice Caraway, fennel, chervil, marjoram
Sharks Fin	Fresh ginger Crab meat Sherry
Spinach (hot)	Sour cream, Ayrshire cream cheese Chives, Basil, chervil, marjoram
Spinach (cold)	Cucumber
Tomato Bouillon	Salted whipped cream, sour cream, Ayrshire cream cheese Allspice, nutmeg Basil, oregano, thyme
Tomato, Cream of	Cream, Ayrshire cream cheese, salted whipped cream Paprika, curry powder Tarragon, basil Anchovy paste
Turkey	Sage Port
Turtle, Green	Chopped hard-boiled egg Basil, lemon slices Sherry
Turtle, Mock	Diced hard-boiled eggs Allspice
Vegetable	Pesto sauce (see page 146) Allspice, curry powder, mace Bay, parsley, basil, thyme
Vichysoisse (cold)	Thick cream Chives
Vichysoisse (hot)	Chives

SECTION TWO

Fish and Shellfish

Fish, probably the most important source of food protein that we have, lends itself to various methods of preservation. It comes to us deep frozen, salted, smoked and dried, in tins and in jars. Although undoubtedly there is nothing to beat fresh fish cooked and eaten almost the moment after it has been caught, some preserved fish—caviare and smoked salmon, for instance, and even humble smoked haddock and kipper—are delicacies in themselves. In this section there are notes under each heading, but there are some general remarks to add. All fish in tins, however preserved—in brine or in oil—tend to be much softer than when fresh; therefore tinned fish needs very little doing to it to make it edible, usually just the addition of a good sauce. Frozen fish also loses a little texture and some flavour in processing, and usually needs a good sauce to replace these things. The textures of salted and smoked fish are part of their attraction, and except for removing excess salt by soaking when necessary, they should be left alone.

All kinds of shellfish are sold in tins and jars, and they can be cooked according to the many recipes in general cookery books for fresh shellfish. Delicatessen shellfish are extremely useful where a recipe calls for a small amount of fish, or where it is not available fresh locally. Paella (see page 109) contains mussels, calamares, shrimps and other fish, all of which can be bought in tins or jars. Many people do worry about the freshness of shellfish, notorious for causing stomach upsets if it is in the least 'off'. Shellfish in tins and jars is completely reliable in this respect.

Frozen fish are also excellent, and are almost exact substitutes for their fresh equivalents.

BOMBAY DUCK, BUMMALOO FISH

Not duck at all but a species of small fish from the Indian ocean. It comes dried in boxes and is an excellent accompaniment to curry. But it has to be cooked before use. It has a pungent smell when cooked so do it well before your guests arrive or you serve your curry, in order to give the smell time to disperse. Put pieces of fish on a baking tin and cook them quickly at the top of a hot oven till they curl at the edges and go golden brown. Remove from the oven and cool. They should be crisp and curled, and can be crumbled over curry at the time of eating. Serve as a side dish.

CAVIARE

Made from the roes of Russian or Persian sturgeon, caviare varies in price according to its source and quality. There are plenty of cheap imitations which come from lumpfish rather than sturgeon, pink in colour, and originating in Canada. Real Russian caviare does not keep very long once the jar is opened.

Caviare is usually served, sprinkled with lemon juice, on small plain biscuits or croûtons of fried bread as hors d'oeuvre. Russians love it with blini (see page 100), and having gone to the expense of buying caviare, it is worth while taking the time and trouble to make these yeast pancakes, to make it go just that bit further.

Devilled Caviare

Stale bread	1 tspn lemon juice
2 tbspn caviare	1 pinch curry powder
½ beef stock cube	1 pinch cayenne pepper

Put all the ingredients except the bread into a small double saucepan and stir well. Heat, but do not boil, and use the mixture to fill croûtons made as follows:

Cut rounds of bread about 2 inches in diameter and 1 inch thick. Then take out the centres a ¼ inch deep, so that you have a bread case. Fry these in hot oil, or oil and butter. Serve either hot or cold.

Special Russian Salad

Caviare	Truffles
Lobster	Gherkins
Anchovy fillets	Capers
Lean ham	Mushrooms
Spring carrots	Beetroot
New potatoes	Spring onions
French beans	Parsley
Peas	Mayonnaise (see page 143)

Cook the carrots, potatoes, spring onions, beans and peas carefully till they are just tender, and sauté the mushrooms lightly in butter. Dice the carrots, potatoes and mushrooms and mix them together. Add chopped truffles (as much or as little as you can afford!), gherkins, capers, and the lobster meat, and ham and anchovy fillets cut into big pieces.

Bind all this together with plenty of mayonnaise and heap it in the middle of a dish. Garnish it all round with diced beetroot, spring onions, parsley and caviare, and serve it with rye bread, or crispbread, and plenty of butter.

CLAMS

Tinned clams can be cooked and served by any recipe designated for oysters or mussels. But clam chowder is a classic shellfish soup which deserves its own recipe.

Clam Chowder

½ lb salt pork or unsmoked bacon	2 pints chicken stock or milk
2 tins clams	½ pint cream
1 onion	2 skinned and seeded tomatoes
2 sticks celery	2 potatoes
1 green pepper	Thyme
1 tbspn flour	Parsley
Butter	Butter

Peel and boil the potatoes, but do not overcook them. Dice them. Dice the pork and cook it in a little butter with the diced onion. Soften, but do not colour. Then add the diced celery and pepper, and stir in a tablespoonful of plain flour as the mixture continues to cook slowly. When the celery and peppers are also soft add the stock or milk, bring it to the boil and add the diced tomatoes and the potatoes. Boil all gently together, and when they too are just cooked, add the chopped clams and then some of the liquor from the tin, tasting the soup as you add it to be sure the liquor does not overpower the soup. Allow the lot to simmer for 15 minutes until the clams are done. Add the cream, but do not let it boil again. Serve garnished with a little thyme and parsley, and with water biscuits.

This soup can be varied by using stock instead of milk, but the soup will be thinner and not so rich.

The proportions of the main ingredients can also be varied slightly to your own taste.

CRAYFISH

Allow frozen crayfish tails to thaw. The central portion of the fan-shaped tail with its attached black spinal cord should not be eaten, and should be removed if it is still there.

Crayfish in Wine Sauce

Crayfish	Bay leaf
Butter	Parsley
White wine	Plain flour
Thyme	Salt and pepper

Heat some butter in a heavy pan and sauté the crayfish in it until they change colour to golden brown. Season with salt and pepper. Transfer to a shallow fireproof dish and cover the fish with dry white wine. Put on the lid and cook in a hot oven for 15 minutes. Drain but keep the stock. Boil it down by half. Make a roux with 1 oz butter and ½ oz flour and add the stock to this, stirring all the time. Pour it over the crayfish, and garnish with parsley. Serve with plain boiled rice.

FROGS' LEGS

We British are a bit doubtful about frogs' legs, for no real reason. They are imported in tins and jars and make an unusual tit-bit for those who fancy them. The simplest way to cook them is to dry them, and then dip them in seasoned flour and then in breadcrumbs, and sauté them in butter. Serve with chopped parsley and lemon juice.

To make them more tasty season them with salt and pepper and sauté them in a covered pan, in butter and a little white wine, then add enough thick Béchamel Sauce (see page 140) to cover them, a few drops of lemon juice and a couple of spoonsful of thick cream. Simmer them for a few minutes longer before serving with an extra knob of butter on each portion, and garnish with slices of lemon and chopped tarragon.

Frogs' Legs au Gratin

Frogs' legs	Cream
Salt and pepper	White wine
Butter	Lemon juice

Cook as above in Béchamel sauce, then put the lot in a fireproof dish. Sprinkle with a layer of breadcrumbs, add a few knobs of butter and brown well in the oven.

HERRINGS (*Salted or Pickled, Dry salted, or in tins or jars*)

Herrings are hard cured by being packed in layers of dry salt, in barrels. These must be soaked overnight in fresh water, milk, or strained tea to remove excess saltiness before they can be eaten. *Matjes* are young herring, which have high oil content, and are lightly cured in fine salt. It may be necessary to wash matjes to remove salt, as the varieties imported into this country will have been well pickled so as not to be too perishable. *Bismarck Herrings* are whole fillets of marinated salt herrings. *Rollmops* are fresh herrings rolled and filled with chopped onion and gherkin and covered in special pickle. *Gaffelbiter* are very salt and sweet marinated herring pieces canned in various sauces. These latter are usually eaten as they are, as an hors d'oeuvre.

Herring Canapés

Salted herrings make excellent cocktail snacks. Cut fillets into inch long pieces (having first soaked, drained and dried them if they are too salty). Make a garnish of sour cream with finely chopped dill, parsley and spring onion, and spread this on small pieces of buttered pumpernickel (see page 98). Put a piece of herring on each small slice.

Marinaded Fillets of Herring on Brown Bread

Stale brown bread	Cayenne pepper
Fillets of herring	Olive oil
White wine	Tarragon vinegar
Butter	Watercress
Parsley	

Cut slices of brown bread about 3/4 inch thick, and toast them. Butter on one side and place on them fillets of herring marinaded in white wine. If you cannot buy these ready marinaded, then use ordinary salted fillets, soaked to remove excess salt. Lay the fillets in a dish and pour over them sufficient wine to cover them, and leave them standing overnight. Lay these fillets on the toast, skin side up, put the slices on a buttered baking tin or shallow dish, cover with buttered paper and cook in a moderate oven for 5 minutes. Remove and cut the slices into fingers, sprinkle alternate fingers with parsley or cayenne pepper, and garnish with watercress and sprinkled with olive oil and tarragon vinegar.

Russian Herring Salad

4 oz mushrooms	Parsley
4 oz new potatoes	4 fillets salt herring
4 oz beetroot	4 tbspn olive oil
4 oz pickled cucumber or gherkin	1 tbspn wine vinegar
	1/2 tbspn dry mustard
4 oz celery or celeriac	Salt and pepper

Put the herrings to soak overnight. Next day cook the mushrooms lightly in butter and slice them, cook the new potatoes and slice them, slice the cooked beetroot and the cucumber, and chop the celery. Mix all these ingredients together carefully. Drain and dry the herrings and place them on a flat dish with the salad arranged round them. Make a dressing with oil and vinegar, mustard and salt, and pour it over the salad, Garnish with plenty of parsley.

Savoury Fillets of Herring

2 herring fillets	FOR THE PURÉE
Butter	½ tin anchovy fillets
Brown bread	1 tbspn thick Béchamel sauce
Dry mustard	(see page 140)
Yolk of hard-boiled egg	2 hard-boiled egg yolks
Cayenne pepper	1 oz butter
	Cayenne pepper

Make a purée by pounding together all the purée ingredients. Soak the fillets to remove excess salt.

Cut a thick slice of brown bread for each serving and toast it. Butter it well and sprinkle dry mustard on it. Spread a good layer of the purée on top of this and lay fillets of herring close together on top again.

Butter a piece of greaseproof paper and place the slices on a baking tin, covering them with paper. Cook in a moderate oven for 10 minutes. Remove from the oven and slice the fillets across with a sharp knife. Sprinkle the rubbed hard-boiled egg yolk and put a dusting of cayenne pepper on each slice. Serve very hot.

Swedish Hors-d'oeuvre

2 fillets salt herring	Lemon juice
Half a cucumber	Caster sugar
1 large onion	

Soak and wash the fillets well and remove the skin. Chop all the ingredients very small, including the fish, and mix lightly together, season with lemon juice and a little caster sugar to taste.

Swedish Matje Salad

2 fillets matjes	2 oz diced beetroot
2 oz sour cream	Parsley
2 hard-boiled eggs	Vinegar
Half a cucumber	Dill
2 oz mayonnaise (see page 143)	

Lay the fillets on a dish and make diagonal cuts half an inch apart through the fillets. Mix the sour cream and the mayonnaise together and spread it round the fish. Garnish with egg whites and yolks separately chopped, diced cucumber sprinkled with dill, diced beetroot sprinkled with vinegar, and chopped parsley.

MUSSELS

Tinned mussels are not pickled in vinegar, so can be used instead of fresh mussels.

Mussels au Gratin

Mussels	Parsley
White breadcrumbs	Salt
Garlic	Olive oil

Drain the mussels and put them in a shallow dish. Sprinkle with breadcrumbs and chopped garlic (to taste), and chopped parsley. Season with salt and sprinkle olive oil all over the breadcrumbs, but don't drench them. Brown the dish in a hot oven (which will dry it out a little), or under a grill if you like it moist.

Mussels in Anchovy Sauce

1 tin mussels	1 wineglass wine vinegar
Olive oil	2 tbspn chopped parsley
1 clove garlic	Black pepper
4 chopped anchovy fillets or 1 tbspn anchovy sauce or paste	½ tspn capers
	2 shallots or spring onions
1 wineglassful dry white wine or dry white vermouth	2 tbspn mayonnaise (see page 143)

Put the mussels in a pan with the wine or vermouth, half the parsley and the onions. Cook together for about 5 minutes. Add to the mayonnaise all the other ingredients. Drain the mussels but retain the juice in which they were cooked and reduce it to 3 tablespoonsful before straining it into the mayonnaise mixture. Add the mussels to the sauce and serve.

Mussel Pizza

Use mussels instead of anchovies to garnish pizza.

OCTOPUS, CALAMARES, SQUID AND CUTTLEFISH

Octopus is a very popular fish in Mediterranean countries, where it is an ingredient of mixed dishes—paella (see page 109), and others. It can be bought here in tins in its own ink sauce, pickled in oil, stuffed, or in other sauces. The preparation of fresh octopus, which can occasionally be bought here, is a little tedious as it must be soaked in running fresh water after it has been cleaned, and the flesh beaten, particularly of larger ones, to make it tender enough to eat. Therefore the tinned variety is, from our point of view, much more convenient, especially as one probably only needs a small amount at a time. The tentacles are usually cut into chunks or stuffed according to the recipe. The flesh is blanched and even after beating, has the texture of rubber. Although many consider it a delicacy, others find it totally inedible!

Large octopus must be boiled before use, but the small ones may be tender enough to grill or fry after blanching, without further boiling.

To clean the fish, remove the insides from the body sac and also the transparent backbone. Remove the purplish outside skin, which will peel off in warm water. Take the ink bags from each side of the head, take out the eyes and the beak, which is in the centre of the tentacles. Rinse under running water until the flesh is milky white. Beat it hard with a steak mallet. If you still fancy it, blanch the flesh by dropping it into boiling salted water for 5 minutes.

Boiled Octopus with Rice

Octopus	Bouquet garni
Onion	Parsley
Olive oil	Rice
White wine	Saffron
Garlic	Lemon juice

Having cleaned, tenderised and blanched the octopus, which should be in pieces, sauté it with the chopped onion until the onion is golden and soft. Then add enough white wine and water in equal quantities, just to cover the fish, a crushed clove of garlic, and a bouquet garni. Cook this by simmering very slowly until the fish is just tender. Add more water and wine if necessary, and transfer it all to a casserole with ½ lb long grain rice and a pinch of saffron, and salt and a squirt of lemon juice. Let it cook in the oven until the rice is tender and all the liquid has been absorbed. Serve sprinkled with chopped parsley, and boiled or creamed spinach.

Octopus and Pasta

tin octopus or calamares, not in sauce	Salt
	2 cloves crushed garlic
1 tin or ½ lb tomatoes	⅓ pint olive oil
2 tbspn chopped parsley	½ wineglass white wine

Sauté the octopus pieces in the oil until they are soft, add the other ingredients and sauté them together until they have formed a thick sauce, and pour this over pasta (see page 112).

Battered Calamares

Cut the fish into pieces and boil until tender as above. Then dip the pieces into thick batter and fry in deep oil until nicely browned.

Stuffed Squid

Several small squid	Bread
Tomatoes	Olive oil
Garlic	Milk
Onion	Béchamel sauce (see page 140)
Parsley	Breadcrumbs
Egg	

Chop the tentacles, the onion and the tomato finely and season them with salt, pepper and a little lemon juice, and fry them in oil. Soak half a small white loaf, without crusts, in milk, and squeeze it dry. Chop the parsley and garlic and mix it with the bread into the contents of the frying pan, stir in 2 egg yolks, and remove immediately from the heat. Adjust the amount of bread, or add a little water to achieve a fairly thick stuffing. Nearly fill the body sacs of the squid with this mixture, and sew each one up. Sauté them in butter.

Sauce: make some thick Béchamel sauce (see page 140) and add to it a little white wine, some finely chopped fried onion. Put the stuffed squid into a fireproof dish and pour the sauce over them, sprinkle the top with breadcrumbs, and brown it in the oven.

Cuttlefish in Soy and Sugar Sauce

1 tin cuttle fish in sauce	1 lemon
1 tin bean sprouts	Plain boiled rice

This is a rather sweet sauce to many tastes, and the addition of a tin of drained bean sprouts, and a little lemon juice absorbs and counteracts some of the sweetness. Combine the contents of the tins and serve on a bed of plain boiled rice garnished with lemon slices. To make more of a meal, serve it with a plain omelette.

OYSTERS AND SCALLOPS

Preserved oysters can be used in any recipe which does not require their being served in the shell, and for any recipe containing cooked oysters, oyster sauces, etc.

Grilled Oysters à La Virginie

1 tin oysters	Butter
2 shallots	3 tbspn Sauce Espagnol (see
1 tbspn parsley	page 146) or ½ pint stock
2 oz mushrooms	½ lb tomatoes
1 egg	Lemon juice
Browned breadcrumbs	

Sauté the sliced tomatoes. Drain the oysters. Chop the shallots, mushrooms and parsley finely together and roll the oysters in them. Pour melted butter over the oysters and dip each one in beaten egg and then in breadcrumbs. Grill for about 5 minutes until nicely browned and serve on the bed of sliced tomatoes.

Mix together the sauce éspagnol (or stock) and some of the oyster liquor and a few drops of lemon juice, bring to the boil, and pour round the tomatoes.

Oysters in Batter

Mince or chop the oysters and mix them with batter, and drop spoonfuls into hot fat. Serve with slices of lemon and brown bread and butter and sauce tartare (see page 147).

Oyster Soufflé

2 oz butter	¼ pint oyster liquor
2 oz plain flour	1 dssrtspn lemon juice
Pinch of salt	Wineglass dry white wine
Pinch of cayenne pepper	5 egg whites, stiffly beaten
3 egg yolks	2 doz oysters, without beards

Put into a double saucepan the butter, flour, pepper and salt and stir well together. Add the egg yolks and the liquids. Stir this mixture until it is just coming to the boil and is thickening. Add the oysters cut into pieces. Butter a soufflé dish and place a band of well buttered paper standing up about 3 inches round the outside. Pour the soufflé mixture into it and stand it in a pan containing water to about ¾ the depth of the soufflé dish. Watch the water re-boil and then let it continue to simmer so that the soufflé steams for 40 minutes. Remove the paper and replace it with a folded napkin, and sprinkle the soufflé with cayenne pepper and chopped parsley. Serve at once.

Scallops

1 tin scallops	1 tbspn brandy
1 small onion	Butter
1 wineglass dry white wine	Salt and pepper
1 dssrtspn chopped parsley	Browned breadcrumbs
1 oz white breadcrumbs	Duchesse potatoes

Melt an ounce of butter in a heavy saucepan and soften in it the chopped onion. Add the scallops, each one cut into four. After a few moments add the wine and brandy together. Heat to boiling point, add the white breadcrumbs and parsley and simmer for 5 minutes.

Divide the mixture into separate individual ovenproof dishes or scallop shells if you have them. Sprinkle browned breadcrumbs over the top and pour a little melted butter on to each. Pipe a border of duchesse potatoes round the edge of each, and brown under a hot grill.

Seafood Casserole

1 tin scallops
1 tin lobster
1 tin prawns
1 tin white fish balls
1 tin mussels (not in vinegar)
¼ lb shallots or onions
Butter
Wineglass dry white wine

½ lb sliced mushrooms
Salt and pepper
1 pint thick Béchamel sauce (see page 140)
Rice or saffron rice (see page 111)
Lemon
Cucumber

Sauté the shallots and mushrooms in butter. Drain all the tins of fish carefully. (Retain the juices if required for fish soup, etc.) Put all the ingredients together in a casserole or ovenproof dish and heat through in a hot oven until the mixture begins to bubble. Make a heap of rice on a dish, and pour the contents over it, or make a border of rice round a big plate and pour the seafood into the middle. Garnish with parsley and slices of lemon and cucumber, and serve with hot bread.

SMOKED SALMON

This is usually eaten as it is with lemon and thin brown bread and butter.

Smoked Salmon Canapés

Spread very thin slices of salmon with cream cheese, season the cheese with either chopped cucumber, horseradish, chopped chives or parsley.

Roll half-inch strips of salmon round small pickled gherkins. There is also a type of marinated salmon known as *Gravlax*. This is marinated in a brandy, beer and dill mixture, and it originates from Scandinavia. It is served in the same way as smoked salmon, or as a main course, if you feel very extravagant, with lemon slices, mustard and dill sauce (see page 144), rye bread and cucumber salad.

Smoked Salmon with Eggs

Slices of pumpernickel or volkornbrot
Slices of smoked salmon

Poached eggs
Dried dill

Dip the slices of salmon into boiling water, drain quickly and dry them, and place them on buttered bread. Put two poached eggs on each slice and sprinkle with dried dill. Serve at once.

SNAILS

These can be bought in cans or jars, in their shells, with the shells supplied separately, or without shells. These snails have only to be put back into their shells with seasoning and cooked briefly, no complicated preparation is needed as with fresh live snails.

Parsley and Garlic Butter for One Dozen Snails

Chop a tablespoonful of fresh parsley very fine, wash it and squeeze it quite dry. Chop and crush half a clove of garlic until it is almost a liquid. Add this to 3 oz of fresh butter, and blend together with a little pepper and nutmeg. Put a little butter in the bottom of each shell, then put in the snail and fill the shells to the top with the garlic butter. Pack the snails in a dish so that they will stay upright while being cooked. If you do not have a special dish for this purpose, use mashed potato or cooked rice in a small shallow dish, and embed the snails firmly in this. Put a piece of baking foil over the dish and cook in a hot oven 450 deg. (gas 8) for 8 to 10 minutes.

To make it easy to eat snails you really do need snail tongs and forks, the one to hold each shell and the other to pick out the snail. These and the cooking dishes and pots can be bought in this country from specialist suppliers, and the kitchen departments of good stores.

TARAMASALATA

This should be made from tarama, the salted and pressed roe of cod or grey mullet, which can be bought at Greek delicatessen, but it can be made quite successfully with tinned cods roe, with salt added.

Taramasalata with salad makes an excellent first course, or on pieces of toast, an unusual hors d'oeuvre. If you like it very creamy, use less bread and less potatoes.

4 oz tarama, or cods roe
1 tbspn grated onion
1 small boiled potato or its equivalent in reconstituted dried)

1 slice stale bread, 2 inches thick
Juice of 2 lemons
¼ pint olive oil
Salt if necessary

Soak the tarama in water to remove salt, but this is not necessary when using fresh or tinned roes. Remove the crust from the bread, dip it in water and squeeze it dry. Put the onion into a blender or pound it until it is a pulp and add the roes. Continue blending until the mixture is creamy. Add the potato and the bread and continue blending all the time. Now, just as if you were making mayonnaise, add a few drops of lemon juice and oil, in a slow stream beating or blending constantly. The mixture should be very light and smooth and faintly pink. You will probably need a little practice before getting this concoction to your liking, as the amount of potato and bread added does alter the consistency so much, and this really is a matter of taste.

TROUT

Deep freezing has made trout available to us all, and it can be cooked by any standard trout recipe. Many people prefer it just slashed across the sides, spread with butter, and grilled, but for something different, try the following:

Trout with Cream and Almonds

Flour
2 oz butter
2 tbspn double cream

1 oz roasted almonds
Salt and pepper
2 trout

Allow the fish to thaw out. Coat them with flour, and sauté them for 5 minutes on each side in the butter in a heavy pan. Season with salt and pepper and put them on a hot serving pan. Add the cream and the almonds cut into slivers to the butter in the pan, stir it all together and heat and pour over the fish.

SECTION THREE

Meat, Sausages, Game and Poultry, and Pâté

As game may only be shot in this country when the law allows, it can only be bought fresh at certain times of the year. It is also very expensive, especially for those living alone. So if you want to eat pheasant, for instance, out of season, or don't want to eat a whole pheasant, how better to buy it than in a tin. Unless of course you are fortunate enough to have a deep freeze with a pheasant in it! The producers of speciality tinned foods of this kind go to a lot of trouble to make their expensive products palatable, in excellent sauces, with good ingredients; but however good, they can usually do with a bit of touching up, or are best used as a basis for a meal, rather than as a complete meal in themselves. This applies to all good quality tinned meat, game and poultry, and the recipes here are almost entirely concerned with using these products in this way.

To use tinned meat, poultry or game, which is of course already cooked, can be very time saving when it comes to making up dishes which require these things as a main ingredient—Coq au Vin, for instance, made from whole cooked chicken.

Venison has recently become much more easily obtainable from ordinary butchers, especially in certain areas, as the farming of deer in parkland has caught on, so some recipes for cooking fresh venison are included as well as some for tinned meat. It does need to be cooked a little differently from the butchers' meat we are used to, so I think comes within the scope of this book.

There are dozens of different types of preserved sausage, coming from all the countries of Europe. Britain has been alone among European countries in developing a very limited range of preserved sausages, usually very local. The Continental sausages are imported here in great numbers, but apart from eating them sliced as a salad or hors d'oeuvre ingredient, we make little use of them. We rarely bother with boiling sausages of different types added to soup and vegetable dishes, or slicing sausage added to pasta, pulses, lentils, peas, chick peas, beans, etc. Yet dried, salted or smoked sausages are more often than not made from poorer cuts of meat, and use up odds and ends, so are, in their countries of origin, cheaper than fresh meat on or off the bone, and they do provide tasty protein to help to balance diets which would otherwise be much too starchy or full of carbohydrates. I can only list here a few of the many sausages, with some of their uses. To try to describe the variation of flavour is impossible; most sausage is full of taste, strong, not subtle, often primarily that of garlic, smoke and salt overlying pork or beef, with a touch of spice or herb as the case may be. You just have to find the ones you like by experimentation.

Also mentioned in this section are a few cooked meat dishes obtainable in tins, such as haggis, with some information as to type of dish and how to cook it out of the tin.

BEEF BOURGUIGNONNE

The extra ingredients which can be added to this dish to stretch it a bit are exactly the same as those for jugged hare (see page 44).

CASSOULET

Poor cassoulet is just a French version of pork and beans, but good cassoulet should contain boiling sausage, pork, mutton and goose, as well as beans, herbs and seasonings. Empty the contents of the tin into a small fireproof dish, and sprinkle a thick layer of breadcrumbs on top. Put it into a moderate oven until the cassoulet is heated through and the breadcrumbs beginning to brown. Stir the breadcrumbs into the cassoulet and add another layer. When this second layer has browned, the dish is ready to serve.

GOULASH

Goulash—meat cooked in paprika sauce—is a favourite tinned meal, because it only requires heating to be ready to serve, and is very highly flavoured. Serve with potatoes and green vegetables or a green salad, or with small suet dumplings which should be cooked in the goulash as it is heating up.

Dumplings for Goulash

Suet   Salt and pepper
S.R. flour

Mix together 2 oz shredded suet with 4 oz flour and a pinch of salt and pepper, moisten with warm water until the mixture makes a very stiff dough. Divide the dough into golf ball sized pieces and roll into balls. Empty the goulash into a saucepan and bring it to the boil, and drop in the dumplings. Continue to simmer for about ¼ hour until the dumplings are cooked through. If the goulash is a little dry, add beef stock made with a stock cube.

Spatzle (see page 115) go well with goulash.

HAGGIS

Although it is as common as sausages north of the border, fresh haggis is only occasionally obtainable outside Scotland, but it can be bought tinned. A haggis is made from oatmeal, suet, meat and the internal organs of a sheep, packed into the sheep's stomach for cooking. To cook a haggis, prick the bag and boil it for 2 hours, if it has not been precooked. Precooked haggis should only be cooked for about ½ hour. It is best eaten with a plain green vegetable or root vegetables. Tinned haggis is an excellent substitute and should be cooked according to the instructions on the tin.

POULTRY AND GAME

Chicken or Turkey a la King

This dish, which is usually made from good left-over pieces of poultry can equally well be made from fowl canned in its own juices.

To each ¾ lb diced poultry meat:
4 tbspn butter
2 level tbspn flour
Crushed bay leaf
Pinch salt, pepper and nutmeg
⅓ pint top of the milk or tinned milk
2 tbspn salad cream
¼ pint thick cream
1 small chopped green pepper
3 oz chopped mushrooms
1 small chopped red pepper
Wineglassful sweet sherry or dry Madeira

Melt half the butter in a saucepan then blend in the flour to make a roux, stir in the top of the milk slowly till the sauce thickens, and add the seasonings. Mix in the salad cream and the cream, stirring all the time so that you achieve a thick smooth sauce. Add the diced chicken or turkey.

Sauté the chopped peppers and mushrooms in the rest of the butter until tender, add these to the sauce, then stir in the sherry. Serve with rice cooked in the juices retained from the chicken, with a little water added, so that when the rice is done all the liquid should be absorbed.

Coq au Vin (1)

Tinned Coq au Vin can of course just be heated up and served as it is, which takes perhaps 10 minutes as opposed to about 2 hours to make from scratch. Nevertheless by adding more of the basic ingredients one can stretch the contents of tins and improve them, without stretching the cooking time too far.

As always when touching up tins of prepared food, it is not necessary to have *all* the extra ingredients mentioned here; even one of them will help a little.

1 rasher lean bacon
1 small onion
2 oz mushrooms
Little butter
Croûtons of bread fried in butter (see page 16)
Pinch nutmeg
Salt and pepper
Red wine

Cook the chopped rasher of bacon, the chopped onion and the mushrooms together in a pan in a little butter, while the chicken is heating in a small covered casserole. When these ingredients are softened but not browned, add them to the contents of the casserole. If the sauce is a little thick or not over-generous, add a tablespoonful of red wine and let it cook for a few minutes longer in the oven. Serve with croûtons and a fresh green salad.

Coq au Vin (2)

1 tin whole chicken	Bouquet garni of thyme, rosemary and bayleaf
½ bottle red wine	
1 tbspn brandy	1 oz butter
1 tbspn plain flour	1 tbspn olive oil
4 oz rashers pork belly	Pinch nutmeg
10 shallots	1 clove garlic
4 oz button mushrooms	Salt and pepper

Open the tin of chicken and put the contents into a saucepan and heat them until you can pour off all the gravy into another saucepan. Continue to heat the chicken gently to dry it out a bit and then remove the breast meat from the bones and skin. Keep the legs and wings whole if possible. Put the skin and carcase into the saucepan of gravy and return it to the stove to simmer and reduce while you get on with the next bit. Chop the pork small and fry it until it begins to get crisp and render its fat. Add the whole shallots and the mushrooms. When the shallots are 'melted' but not brown, add the chicken pieces and continue to cook for a few minutes. As soon as the chicken is heated through add the brandy and light it.

When the flames have gone right out, add the wine, the bouquet garni, crushed garlic, and nutmeg and salt and pepper to taste. Bring the whole lot to the boil and transfer it to a heated casserole. Put the casserole in the oven and cook it at 425 (gas 7) for 10 minutes and 350 (gas 4) for a further 15. Meanwhile make a roux with the flour and a little butter. By now the stock should be well reduced, add enough of it to the roux, stirring all the time to make a very thick sauce. Just before serving, add this to the contents in the casserole, blending well and adding stock to get the gravy to the exact consistency you like.

Tinned chicken tends to fall to pieces, so throughout, try to handle the meat carefully, so that it does stay on the legs and wings at least. Serve with plenty of croûtons of fried bread and a green vegetable.

Duck in Orange Sauce

1 tin whole roast duck with orange sauce	½ wineglass dry white wine
	1 tbspn Grand Marnier
1 thinly sliced sweet orange	Boiled rice (see page 108)

Heat up the bird in its tin according to instructions, then drain the sauce into a bowl and slide the bird very carefully on to a serving dish which can be put into a low oven for a few moments, while you improve the sauce.

Add the wine and Grand Marnier to the sauce, more or less to taste, and bring it quickly to the boil. As soon as it boils remove it from the heat and pour it over the bird. Garnish the dish with slices of fresh orange, and serve at once with plain boiled rice.

Grouse

Whole roast grouse in tins should be served in exactly the same way as Quail (see page 44), substituting wine for sherry.

Partridge

This can be cooked by any of the recipes for pheasant (see pages 43-44) or quail (see page 44).

Partridge with Mushrooms

¼ lb mushrooms per bird	Stock
1½ oz butter	2 wineglasses sherry
1½ oz plain flour	Salt and pepper

Heat the birds in the tin until the juices can be poured into a bowl. Sauté the mushrooms with plenty of pepper and salt. Stuff the body cavity of the bird with this and put it in a moderate oven for 10 minutes in a fireproof dish while you make the sauce.

Add the sherry to the juices in the bowl, and extra stock if there is not enough to make a good serving of gravy. Melt the butter in a saucepan and mix the flour with it to make a roux, then slowly add the gravy, stirring all the time. When the consistency is right, allow it to cook for a few minutes more. Remove the bird from the oven, pour the sauce over it and serve it at once with plain boiled rice and green vegetables.

Madeira Pheasant

1 whole tinned pheasant
2 slices chopped ham
1 chopped onion
1 stick chopped celery
1 oz butter
1 wineglassful Madeira
Stock (if necessary)

Put all the ingredients to sauté in butter, except the Madeira, stock and pheasant. Transfer the contents of the tin to a small casserole and when the vegetables and ham are soft, put them round the pheasant. Pour the Madeira and stock over the lot, put on the lid and cook in a medium oven till everything is well heated through. Serve with croûtons of fried bread (see page 16).

Roast Pheasant

1 tin roast pheasant
Butter
Flour
Red wine
Bread sauce (see page 156)
Breadcrumbs or game chips
Few rashers of bacon

Heat the pheasant in its tin for a few minutes so that the gravy can be poured off into a bowl. Transfer the bird carefully to a small covered fireproof dish, and pour some melted butter over the bird. Put it in a medium oven to heat through, and if the skin is not browned, remove the lid of the dish and cook for a further 15 minutes. Meanwhile improve the gravy by adding a little red wine, and thicken it if necessary with a roux of butter and flour. Make some bread sauce and fry some breadcrumbs in butter, or make game chips by cooking thinly sliced potatoes in very hot oil, and fry several rashers of bacon till crisp. Serve the bird with these garnishes and green vegetables.

Pheasant with Apples

1 tinned roast pheasant
Butter
8 medium cooking apples
3 tbspn cream
1 wineglassful Calvados
Sugar
Salt and pepper

Melt 4 oz butter in the bottom of an enamel casserole on top of the stove, and sauté the diced peeled apples with a pinch of sugar in this until just soft. Transfer the contents of the tin on to the top of the apples. Mix together the Calvados and cream and pour it over the bird. Put on the lid and heat all together in a moderate oven for 30 minutes. Season with a little salt and pepper and serve with potatoes.

Pigeon

Whole roast pigeon in tins should be served in exactly the same way as Quail, substituting wine for sherry.

Quail in Sherry Sauce

1 tin quail in sherry sauce	Sherry
Thick slice white bread	Lemon wedges
Butter	

Heat up a tin of whole 'Quail in Sherry Sauce' according to the instructions on the tin. Fry a thick slice of white bread in butter. Drain the sauce from the tin into a saucepan, and put the bird on the fried bread on a hot dish on which it is to be served. Bring the sauce just to the boil, add a little sherry, and pour it over the bird and the croûton of bread. Serve with lemon wedges.

HARE AND VENISON

Jugged Hare

Excellent jugged hare can be bought in tins, which just needs heating up and serving with good vegetables, red currant jelly and forcemeat. As with other game it can be improved and stretched by the addition of extra onions and mushrooms sautéed in butter, fried fat diced bacon, and a little extra port wine or Burgundy added to the heated-up hare.

Venison

Some butchers sell frozen venison, and as a meat which is for us unusual, it should come into the scope of this book. It can also be bought tinned. Venison suffers from being very dry meat, so it is excellent when canned because it must of necessity have plenty of sauce with it. Usually canned in red wine, it is of course fine just heated up and served with good vegetables, but to make something more of it, turn it into a Venison Pasty with a rich crust.

Venison Pasty

1 tin venison	Pinch allspice
Beef stock	For the dough:
1 dssrtspn wine vinegar	½ lb flour
1 wineglassful red wine or port	¼ lb butter
1 grated onion	2 eggs
Lemon juice	Hot water
Salt and pepper	

Place the contents of the tin in a fireproof dish and add the vinegar, red wine or port, and some beef stock if there is insufficient. Shred a grated onion on to the top of the meat. Make a dough with the listed ingredients, doubling up the quantities if you need more pastry. Rub the flour and butter together, add the beaten eggs and mix well, and add sufficient hot water to make a good stiff dough. Roll it out 3 times, doubling it between each rolling. The final roll should leave the dough nearly ½ inch thick. Place this on top of the meat and make pastry decorations with the trimmings. Be sure the pastry is sealed well to the edge of the dish to retain moisture.

Cook the pasty in a moderate oven 350/375 deg. (gas 4/5) until the pastry is nicely browned. It may be necessary to moisten the gravy again before serving. Heat a little beef stock and red wine together with a squirt of lemon juice and a dash of salt and pepper and a pinch of allspice, and pour it under the crust.

Venison pasty can of course be made with fresh meat, in which case use the poorer cuts trimmed and boned, and make the stock from the bones. Dice and sauté a rasher of belly pork and add it to the meat, with enough stock to cover, a ¼ pint of port wine, a dash of vinegar, salt and pepper, mace and allspice, and 2 grated onions. Cook altogether in a covered casserole until the meat is tender, and put on the crust and continue as above.

Venison, Roast

The haunch is the best joint for roasting
Allspice
Mace
Salt and pepper
½ pint tarragon vinegar
½ pint claret
¼ lb butter
2 tspn soy sauce
Juice of 3 lemons
Flour

Make a mixture of equal amounts of the spices and salt and pepper, and rub it all over the meat by hand, making sure that it is thoroughly coated. Mix together the lemon juice, vinegar and wine, and pour it over the meat. Leave it to marinate in this for at least half a day, turning it and basting it frequently.

Put the haunch in a covered roasting dish, and mix the marinating liquid with the melted butter, and baste the meat with this while cooking it at 350 deg. (gas 4) for 2 hours or longer according to size. 15 minutes before serving, remove the lid from the tin, baste the meat for the last time, and pour off the gravy into a bowl. Dredge the meat lightly with flour and return it to a high oven for long enough to brown it off thoroughly. Add the soy sauce to the gravy and reheat it ready to serve with the roast meat.

Serve it with buttered noodles, or spatzle (see page 115) and a good mixed salad.

Venison may be stewed and grilled or fried as is beef, but it does tend to be dry, so needs plenty of added fat, either diced belly pork or butter, and plenty of added gravy, usually containing port or claret, a little vinegar and plenty of spices and seasonings.

HAMS AND SAUSAGES

Uncooked Smoked Ham

Kasseler Rippenspeer—German smoked loin of pork, which is absolutely delicious and can be used in any recipe which requires cold ham. Specially good in hors d'oeuvre or smörgåsbrod.

Krajana—Polish ham sausage which also tastes much like our kinds of ham and has the same uses; it is smoked, and roasted by the heat of the smoke room, to its own special flavour.

There are several varieties of European ham which are not cooked by boiling as we do here but are cured and smoked. These usually have a wonderful flavour, but are a little chewy, and must be served cut in paper-thin slices. *Bayonne* and *Parma* produce this kind of ham and there are also several German types: *Lasschinken, NussSchinken, Knochenschinken* and *Bauernschinken.* Some of these 'hams' are from parts of the pig other than the ham, but the general taste and effect is exactly the same. There are slight regional variations in the cure and type of smoking.

Cooking Sausages

Frankfurters (excellent with sauerkraut, see page 74), *Augsburgers,* and French smoked sausages (*Sausages Fumées*), *Weiner Würstchen* (Vienna sausage), *Polnischewürste, Rindfleisch, Kochwürste,* and *Knackwürste,* and what are called simply 'boiling rings' in this country are all cooked by being poached in boiling water for about 10 minutes, and are served hot with various garnishes and vegetables. *Toulouse sausages, Nürnbergers,* and of course English sausages can be grilled or fried.

Saveloys, smoked and spiced sausages from Paris, Lyons and Nancy should also be poached in water and eaten either hot, or cold as hors d'oeuvre.

Cotechino. A lightly salted Italian pork salami which is excellent hot. Steam or simmer it, wrapped in a cloth for 2 hours, remove the skin. Serve it hot with lentils (see page 118) or hot sliced potatoes seasoned with vinaigrette dressing (see page 47). Almost any large sausage can be cooked whole and served in slices. Horseradish sauce makes a good garnish for hot sausage.

Chorizos

These are Spanish cured sausages with chunky cut meat usually packed in ring form in a red wrinkled skin. They can be eaten raw as bought, or casseroled, or stewed with Chick Peas (see page 117). Chorizos can also be added in pieces or thin slices to soups to make more of a meal of them. They are good in lentil or pea soup. Chorizos, gently fried in olive oil, are excellent served with Spanish sauce (see page 148).

Spanish Meat Balls in Sherry Sauce

1 lb finely minced beef
¼ lb Chorizo sausage
Pinch salt
Pinch nutmeg
1 tspn minced parsley
2 slices bread soaked in milk
1 egg
3 tbspn olive oil
¼ pint beef stock
¼ pint sherry

Mix the meats, salt and nutmeg. Squeeze the bread out and add it with the beaten egg to the meat mixture. Form into balls about the size of golf balls, and sauté them in olive oil. Heat the beef stock, add the sherry and pour it over the meat balls. Serve hot.

Slicing Sausages

Salami are dried meat sausages containing highly concentrated and compressed minced pork and sometimes beef. They are very dry and should be thinly sliced for eating, usually as hors d'oeuvre, but keep for a long time if uncut or in the piece. Italian, Hungarian, Belgian, German, Danish and Polish salami all differ slightly in taste and texture.

There are other small dried meat sausages such as these from Arles or Lyons, which are always eaten sliced and raw. These contain meat much more coarsely cut than does salami. Try them with French bread and butter, black olives and a glass of red wine.

On the whole much softer than salami or Cervelat, there are various Polish garlic sausages and German sausages such as *Bierwurst*; Italian sausages such as *Mortadella*, which are usually eaten sliced and uncooked, but are occasionally cooked. Add pieces of *Milan sausage* to minestrone soup.

Cervelat, Cabanos, Landjaeger, Westfälischer, Mettwurst, Plockwurst, Chorizos and many others are also made from chopped smoked and dried meat, but are not quite so hard as salami.

Spreading Sausages

Various kinds of liver sausage; *Teewurst* made of finely minced lean pork, *Braunschweiger* made primarily of pork, and many others intended to be eaten spread on bread and biscuits.

PÂTÉS AND TERRINES

All delicatessen sell pâté, either in tins, polythene tubes, or by the ounce out of earthenware basins (when strictly speaking they become terrines). They can be based on almost any meat, poultry or game, often include liver, wine or spirits, and flavourings such as truffles or juniper. Some are so finely ground as to be the consistency of paste, others have large chunks or strips of meat in them. Pâté on the whole is much richer and more subtly flavoured than sausage, and is usually soft enough to be spread or heaped upon bread, or biscuits, and eaten by itself in that way, or with salad ingredients. Your delicatessen manager should be able to tell you exactly what each of his pâtés is like, and to suggest which would be suitable for your purposes. It is extremely difficult here to give any rules of thumb, as apart from those made by a few well known companies, which are consistent, many delicatessen make up their own pâtés to sell by the ounce, or have them made up locally by a specialist, and these can all differ from batch to batch. Pâté is usually eaten 'straight'.

Baked Potatoes and Pâté

1 baked potato per person	Butter
1 oz pâté of any type per person	Salt and pepper
Any salad	

Scrub and bake a large potato per person, split it lengthwise but not right through, and put inside it a long sliver of butter, and a sprinkling of salt. Fill the opened potato with pâté and serve immediately.

Liver Pâté Dip

6 oz plain liver pâté	Salt and black pepper
3 oz sharp cream cheese	Saltspn nutmeg
2 tbspn salad cream	Tspn curry powder
2 tbspn sherry	1 tbspn cream or top of the milk
1 tbspn Worcestershire sauce	Pinch cayenne

This is a delicious, rather sharp, moist pâté, excellent served with toast melba, crispbread and watercress or celery as a first course, or with plain biscuits as a dip at drinks parties.

Put all the ingredients together in a bowl or blender and mix to a smooth paste. Adjust the seasoning to taste, but do not overdo the curry powder or the pâté will taste of nothing else. It should be barely distinguishable as there at all.

Chill and serve garnished with thinly sliced cucumber.

Quail Eggs Scotched

1 tin quail eggs	Plain flour
Any spreading pâté	Cayenne pepper
Breadcrumbs	Mayonnaise (see page 143)
Beaten egg	

Drain the eggs, and dry them and dip each one in flour so that it has a thin coating. Spread each egg with a complete layer of pâté, as thick as you fancy. Dip it in the beaten egg and then in breadcrumbs and fry in deep hot oil. Leave to cool, cut in halves, sprinkle with cayenne and serve with mayonnaise.

SECTION FOUR

Vegetables

As I said in the Introduction, this book came about because my greengrocer stocks every once-exotic vegetable and fruit he can get. When he began doing this, an awful lot of it went to waste unsold, because his customers were unused to such things. I think the tendency is still to use these vegetables and fruits to make special dishes, or to eat them by themselves with special sauces. This is fine, for when the taste is a new one it is probably the best way to savour it, and most of the things are relatively expensive. But one should not forget to use the vegetables in exactly the same way as one does familiar things like cabbage and carrot, marrow and tomato. Sufficient demand cuts down on percentage of unsold waste, and encourages producers, wholesalers and retailers to provide more, which will certainly stabilise prices and might even bring them down, especially those of fruit and vegetables imported from common market countries.

ARTICHOKE

The Globe Artichoke is a large, thistle-like plant, the flowerhead of which we eat before it blooms (although if left to bloom it is magnificent!). This head consists of fleshy, greyish-green leaves sprouting from a fleshy base, enclosing the 'choke' an inedible hairy bit which would eventually grow out to be the purple flower. The very fleshy bases of the leaves and the fleshy hearts or bottoms are the only parts which are eaten in this country, but all the vegetable except the choke and stalk can be eaten if you can get it young and fresh enough. The Italians boil the heads and then slice them thinly and fry them in butter or batter, and use the vegetable generally just about as much as we do cabbage.

Artichokes have always been known here as a luxury, and there are plenty of recipes in most cookery books, but only recently has it become really plentiful in every greengrocers'.

To prepare them, first soak the globes in cold salted water for an hour to remove dirt and insects. Cut off the stalks at the base of the leaves, pull off tough and dirty outside leaves, and trim the tops down about an inch. Tie the globes round with string to keep them compact and place them base downwards in boiling salted water. When cooked, which takes about half an hour to an hour according to age and size, the leaves pull off easily and the bottoms give slightly when pressed with the thumb. If the vegetable is to be served stuffed or cold the choke must be scooped out with a teaspoon. Open up the centre carefully to get at it.

When artichokes are plentiful and cheap, use only the hearts. Trim the outer leaves very short or remove them, and cut out the choke with a sharp knife. Rub the hearts with lemon before cooking, or soak them briefly in water with added lemon juice, to prevent them from going brown.

Artichoke hearts and bottoms can be bought pickled or in tins ready for use, but are not so tasty as fresh ones.

Various sauces go with hot boiled artichokes; Béchamel, Hollandaise, Mousseline, or melted butter. Mayonnaise, mustard sauce, vinaigrette or tartare sauce improve cold artichokes (see pages 138-150).

Artichoke Hearts with Ham and Cheese Sauce

4 artichokes
2 oz lean ham
¼ pt Béchamel sauce (see page 140)
1 oz grated cheese
black pepper
butter

Prepare the artichokes and cook them until they are just tender. Remove the leaves and fry the hearts in butter for five minutes, then put them in a buttered fireproof dish. Chop the ham and add it to white sauce well seasoned with pepper. Pour the sauce over the artichokes and sprinkle on a layer of cheese, and a few knobs of butter. Cook in a medium oven until the surface is golden brown.

Artichoke Salad

2 artichokes
3 tbspn olive oil
1 tspn wine vinegar
1 dssrtspn chopped parsley
1 tspn dried tarragon
Salt and black pepper
1 chopped shallot

Boil the artichokes until tender, then cut them into quarters and remove the chokes. Arrange the pieces on a dish and make a dressing with the oil, vinegar and seasonings to taste.

Artichokes, stuffed

The centre of the globe, after the choke has been removed, can be filled with any meat or vegetable mixture you like. Tie a piece of bacon round each globe and put them in a buttered fireproof dish and cook in a slow oven until tender, basting frequently.

Meat or vegetable filling	Chicken stock
Butter	Onion
Bacon	Carrots
White wine	Bouquet garni

Chop the bacon onion and carrots and make a layer of them in the bottom of a fireproof dish. Place the globes on this and pour ¼ pint of stock and a wine glassful of white wine over them. Hang in the bouquet garni. Put on a lid and cook in a slow oven for at least an hour, basting frequently. Remove from the oven, drain off the liquor and use it to make a sauce by adding it to a roux of plain flour and butter.

Artichokes Stuffed with Anchovy Bread

3 artichokes	1 chopped clove garlic
1 tbspn breadcrumbs	Wineglass white wine
2 chopped anchovy fillets	Olive oil

Be sure the globes are young and tender. Soak and trim them and remove the choke. Blanch them for 5 minutes in boiling salted water. Mix together the breadcrumbs, anchovy fillets and garlic and with this fill the centres of the vegetables. Use a deep, heavy-based saucepan and put enough oil in it to cover the bottom, heat it and put in the artichokes. Pour in the wine, and simmer the vegetables gently for at least an hour until tender, basting occasionally. Fry small pieces of bread in the remaining oil and liquor, adding more oil if necessary, and serve the artichokes on these croûtons.

Marinated Artichokes

3 artichokes
2 cloves garlic
1 tbspn chopped parsley

Juice of 1 lemon
Salt and pepper

Prepare and boil the artichokes. When tender remove them from the water but keep it. Remove the chokes. Make a marinade with the rest of the ingredients, crushing the garlic thoroughly, and pour this over the artichokes, making sure they are well coated. Leave them for an hour then return them to the pan and simmer them for a quarter of an hour. Let them stand in the saucepan till cool, then drain and serve cold with cold meat.

Shrimp and Artichoke Salad

1 tin, or its equivalent in fresh vegetables of artichoke hearts (6 to 8 oz)
4 oz tin prawns, shrimps, crab or lobster

1 carton natural yoghurt
2 tbspn chopped chives
Salt
Juice of 1 lemon
Lettuce heart

Mix the yoghurt, chives and lemon juice. Dice the artichokes and add them to the yoghurt with some of the liquor from the tin. Add about half the fish. Don't make the sauce too thin. Season it to taste. This will be a very sharp, sour dressing. Put the lettuce on plates and pile the mixture over the lettuce. Use the rest of the fish to garnish and decorate each plate.

AUBERGINES

The shiny purple fruit of the Aubergine or Egg Plant is a common vegetable in Near Eastern and Mediterranean countries. Only recently has it been marketed extensively here. There are several varieties, long or round, small or large, which mature at slightly different times of the year. Aubergine is a soft, sweet-tasting vegetable which has enough flavour to be enjoyed by itself, or mixed with other vegetables, or as a vegetable with meat. It is especially good with mutton.

When the recipe allows, sprinkle the cut aubergine with salt and leave it for at least half an hour in a colander, and then shake and dry it before cooking. This gets rid of a slight

AUBERGINES

bitterness, and makes the vegetable more digestible. It is usually cooked in oil or butter and absorbs a lot in the process, rendering some up again as it cooks and softens. Sliced aubergines burn very easily in the pan at the beginning of frying or sautéing, so take care to keep the gas low. It pays to keep the pan covered to retain moisture and soften the aubergine more quickly. Usually the skin is eaten, but when the recipe demands that it be removed, put the fruit under a grill until the skin chars and wrinkles, when it should peel easily under running water. Aubergines can also be peeled just like potatoes.

In India, where it originated, the aubergine is used as a curry ingredient or as a 'sambal'. In Greece it is a vital ingredient of moussaka—the Greek equivalent of shepherd's pie.

Aubergine Agrodolce

Aubergines can be cooked and served in exactly the same sweet and sour sauce as courgettes, using the same method (see Courgettes, page 64).

Aubergine and Pepper Salad

Lemon juice
2 big aubergines
2 green peppers
2 red peppers
1 clove garlic

1 tbspn chopped parsley
Salt and pepper
¼ pt mayonnaise or tahina
(see pages 143 and 149)

Char and peel the aubergines, slit them and leave them to drain. Mash and pulp them thoroughly, adding lemon juice drop by drop (an electric blender will do this job). Chop one red pepper and one green pepper into dice and stir them into the pulp with the parsley. Stir in the mayonnaise or tahina. Halve the other two peppers and pile the mixture into the halves. This is really two recipes in one as the two sauces impart very different flavours.

Aubergine Fries

Aubergines
Eggs
S.R. flour

Salt and pepper
Frying oil

Peel the aubergines and chop them, and stew the pieces in a

little water till tender. Drain, and mash and mix with beaten egg, in the ratio of 2 cups of aubergine pulp per egg. Add enough flour to make a soft dough which can be formed into balls in the hand. Season to taste. Roll the mixture into balls the size of golf balls, flatten them, and fry them in hot oil until they are brown. Serve with fried bacon or sausage.

Aubergine Purée for Curry

½ lb aubergines
1 small chopped onion
1 tbspn ground coriander
1 tspn ground aniseed
1 tspn chopped parsley
Pinch each paprika, salt
Butter

Scorch the whole fruit thoroughly under a grill and peel it, leaving a few bits to add smoky taste. Mash the aubergine to a smooth purée in a blender. Heat the butter in a heavy pan and soften the onion in it. A teaspoonful of water added from time to time will help this process. Add the spices and the aubergine pulp and cook the mixture fact for a few minutes, stirring all the time to prevent browning and sticking. Then turn the flame right down, cover the pan, and cook for another seven or eight minutes. This is excellent served with curry instead of dahl.

Aubergine Salad

1 medium aubergine
2 spring onions or chives
3 tomatoes
Lettuce
1 tbspn wine vinegar
3 tbspn olive oil
½ tspn caster sugar
Salt and pepper

Bake the aubergine in a moderate oven for about ¾ hour until it is soft. Peel and chop it into cubes. Mix it well with the chopped tomatoes, onions and seasonings, and chill it thoroughly. Serve on crisp lettuce leaves with toast Melba.

Curried Aubergines

2 small aubergines
2 oz butter
2 large sliced onions
1 clove garlic
3 tomatoes
Chicken stock
1 tbspn ground coriander
1 tspn each of ground turmeric, cumin, ginger, mustard, fenugreek
Pinch chilli powder

An unusual vegetable curry good by itself or served with a meat or fish curry as a 'sambal'.

Sauté the onions and garlic in butter until tender, then add spices and fry for 5 minutes without burning. Add chopped tomatoes and aubergines, and cover with stock. Simmer till the aubergine is tender and the gravy thick, but do not over-cook to the point of mushiness.

Fried Aubergines

Aubergines	Olive oil
Flour and water batter	Skorthalia or Avgolemno sauce
1 egg	(see pages 147 and 139)
Salt and pepper	

Slice the aubergines thinly, put them in a colander and salt well. Leave for an hour. Drain and dry. Meanwhile make a batter by beating the egg, adding plain flour till it is the consistency of very thick cream, then diluting it with water until it is that of thin cream. Heat the oil till it is just smoking. Dip each aubergine slice in batter and drop it in the fat. When the batter is browned on both sides, drain and serve with sauce or as a vegetable to accompany lamb chops.

Imam Bayaldi

2 lb aubergines	1 clove garlic
½ pt olive oil	1 tbspn chopped parsley
6 tomatoes	Salt and pepper
4 onions	Thyme
2 tbspns currants	Bay leaf

A fancy name for what is in fact stuffed aubergines. It is supposed to have made an Imam faint with delight the first time he tasted it. It is a good tasty dish, but not as marvellous as all that and one wonders what terrible food the poor man must have been eating before!

Cut the aubergines in half, lengthways, and scoop out the pulp, carefully leaving a little flesh inside the undamaged skins. Sprinkle the halves with salt and leave them to drain for half an hour. Dry them. Meanwhile chop up the pulp, tomatoes, onions and garlic together and fry in oil until just soft. Fill the aubergine halves with the mixture. Pack them into a fireproof dish and cover them with oil, and sprinkle bay leaf and thyme over all. Put the lid on and cook very slowly in a low oven until the oil has been absorbed. Cool, and chill in the fridge and eat it next day. To make the dish quickly, fry the halved skins in olive oil before stuffing, and cook as before for only ¾ hour. This is a very rich oily dish, and not for those who cannot stomach too much oil.

Moussaka

3 sliced aubergines
1 lb minced lamb
2 big onions
3 tbspn tomato purée
1 clove garlic
¼ tspn each, cinnamon, nutmeg, salt, black pepper

Wineglass red wine or water
½ lb grated cheese
3 eggs
¾ pt Béchamel sauce (see page 140)
Olive oil
1 oz butter

Prepare the aubergines, and fry them in hot olive oil until they are browned but not mushy. In another pan melt the butter and sauté the chopped onions until golden. Add the meat and sauté until brown. Add spices, flavourings, tomato purée and wine, and simmer with a lid on for ½ hour. Meanwhile make the sauce, and when the meat is cooked add a spoonful or two of it to thicken the gravy. The mixture should be neither too sloppy nor too dry. Butter well a baking dish with straight sides. Put a layer of aubergine slices at the bottom, then a layer of meat, then a sprinkle of cheese. Continue until all are used up, finishing with aubergines.

Put this in a medium oven for ¼ hour. Meanwhile beat the eggs well and add them to the Béchamel sauce. Pour it all over the meat and aubergines as a topping, sprinkle with more cheese and bake in a medium hot oven for ½ hour or until the top is golden brown.

The result should be firm enough to cut out in chunks, meat and aubergines below a thick topping of custardy sauce and cheese, without collapsing on the plate. On the other hand it must not be a stodgy loaf. Some cooks omit the cheese, others use more aubergine and omit the sauce. Others use veal or minced beef, and artichokes or courgettes instead of Aubergines, but the result is not, strictly speaking, moussaka.

Raw Aubergine Salad

Aubergines
Vinaigrette dressing
(see page 147)
Chervil
Tarragon

Peel the Aubergine and cut it into thin slices and salt it for ½ hour. Drain and dry. Season with vinaigrette dressing and sprinkle a little chervil and tarragon overall.

Stuffed Aubergines au Gratin

Halve the aubergines, make a few slits in them and sprinkle with salt and leave them for an hour. Drain and dry the halves and fry them in hot oil until they are soft but not broken. Scoop out the pulp carefully. Mix it with any of a variety of ingredients before piling it back into the half skins. Pack the halves into a fireproof dish, sprinkle well with plenty of breadcrumbs and/or grated cheese, and with butter and oil, and put it back in the oven to cook and brown.

Additional Ingredients per 1 lb of Aubergines

1. 1 hard-boiled egg, chopped
   1 sautéed chopped onion
   Breadcrumbs
   1 clove garlic
   1 tbspn parsley

   Mix with the pulp and continue as above.

2. 8 oz cottage cheese
   2 eggs
   2 oz hard cheese, grated
   Salt and pepper

   In an electric blender combine the pulp, cottage cheese, eggs and salt and pepper. Fold in the grated cheese and continue as above.

3. 4 oz sausage meat
   2 oz chopped mushrooms
   1 egg
   1 tbspn chopped herbs, mixed tarragon, parsley, chives thyme or marjoram
   Salt and pepper

   Pre-cook the sausage meat without browning it and pour off fat. Mix all the ingredients with the pulp and raw egg, stir well, and continue as above.

4. Lean cooked lamb or mutton
   Boiled rice
   1 clove garlic
   Parsley
   Salt and pepper

   Combine equal amounts of meat and rice, with garlic, parsley, salt, pepper and pulp, and continue as above.

5. ½ lb minced lamb, beef or veal
2 oz mushrooms
4 tbspn chopped celery
Big pinch each turmeric, cumin, cayenne, salt, dried basil

Mix all together and fry in butter for five minutes, stirring constantly. Combine with pulp, and continue as above, omitting cheese.

BAMBOO SHOOTS

A common ingredient of Chinese food. Strain off the liquor before adding the shoots to meat and chicken dishes.

Bamboo Shoots Stir Meat Slices

1 lb lean pork
1 can bamboo shoots
2½ tbspn soy sauce
1 tbspn sherry
2 tbspn vegetable oil
1 tspn sugar
1 tspn salt
1 tbspn cornflour
2 tbspn water

Cut the meat into small thin slices about 1 inch square. Mix together all ingredients except bamboo shoots and salt. Heat the oil in a frying pan and cook the mixture for 3 minutes. Stir all the time to prevent burning. Slice the drained bamboo shoots and salt them and add to the rest. Cook for 3 minutes more. Serve with boiled or fried rice and other Chinese dishes.

Chicken with Bamboo Shoots

1 small chicken
2 oz mushrooms
2 thin slices ginger or piece of dried ginger root
½ tin bamboo shoots
2 cloves garlic
1 tbspn soy sauce
Plain flour
2 tbspn vegetable oil
Salt and pepper
Chicken stock

This dish is best made with green ginger but if this is unobtainable bruise and soak a small piece of root ginger in hot water and put it in with the cooking chicken, removing it before serving. Joint the chicken and cut it into small pieces on the bone, taking care not to splinter the bone. Coat each piece with seasoned flour. Crush the garlic and slice the ginger and fry them in oil until they are brown, then add the mushrooms, cut in large pieces or left whole if they are small. Add the chicken and fry until brown. Remove the lot to a fireproof dish or casserole and add the drained bamboo shoots and enough chicken stock just to cover the meat. Add soy sauce and cook in a medium oven until the chicken is tender. Serve with boiled rice.

If you use chicken stock made up from a cube or powder, cut down on the seasoning added to the flour, or the dish may become too salty.

BEAN SPROUTS

Another common ingredient of Chinese food. Bean sprouts can be bought in tins, but are nothing like so crisp as fresh sprouts.

To cook the vegetable, put them in a pan with a little heated cooking oil, and sauté for two minutes, stirring all the time. Then add a good sprinkling of soy sauce and salt to taste. Cover the pan and cook slowly for five minutes more. Serve as a separate vegetable with Chinese food, or in Spring Rolls and other composite Chinese dishes.

Spring Rolls

Batter
4 oz plain flour
1 oz cornflour

4 eggs
¾ pint water

Mix the flours, break in the eggs and stir in, add enough water to make thin batter. Heat oil in a heavy frying pan and pour in enough batter to cover the pan thinly, tilting the pan to spread the batter. When just cooked, but not browned, remove from the pan and put in the filling. When all the rolls have been made by rolling up the pancake and tucking in the ends, heat a deep panful of peanut oil till it is smoking and deep fry the rolls to golden brown.

Filling These ingredients can be varied according to what is available. Made with all ingredients the roll is a meal in itself; with only bean sprouts and a minimum of meat and fish, and flavourings, it becomes an accompaniment other Chinese dishes.

¼ lb or small tin prawns or shrimps
6 oz lean pork, shredded
1 tin bean sprouts
Chives or spring onions
2 chopped onions

2 cloves garlic
Chopped water chestnuts
1 small turnip, grated
Soy sauce
Sugar
Peanut oil

Heat 4 tablespoonsful of oil in a big heavy frying pan and sauté the onions until they are golden. Put them aside while you cook the pork and prawns in the same oil. Put these with the onions and fry the bean sprouts chives and water chestnuts and garlic. Put this with the other cooked ingredients and fry the turnip for a few minutes. Add just enough water to moisten it and simmer until tender. Stir in soy sauce and sugar to taste and add to the other ingredients.

CELERIAC

A variety of celery which has big edible roots. It tastes almost exactly the same as ordinary celery, but a little more sickly. It is a turnip-like vegetable, and for use must be peeled and cut into slices or chunks which can then be added to stews, or boiled or stewed and served separately as a vegetable. Celeriac can also be shredded and eaten raw as a salad.

Celeriac Cooked in Butter

1 celeriac
Butter

Salt
Water

Peel the celeriac and cut it into small pieces or strips. Put it in a heavy saucepan with butter and a sprinkling of salt. Put enough water in the pan to prevent burning, and cook with the lid on, shaking every few minutes and making sure that the pan does not boil dry. When the water is used up, add a little more, but don't cover the vegetables. The steam from the water and the hot butter soften them quite quickly.

Celeriac Fritters

Celeriac
Frying batter (see page 140)

Cooking oil

Peel the celeriac and boil it for 30 minutes. Then cut it into thin slices, dip each slice in the batter and fry it in hot oil until golden.

Celeriac Salad

Cleaned and shredded celeriac
Mayonnaise (see page 143)
French mustard
Salt and pepper
Cream

Put the shredded celeriac in a bowl and coat it thoroughly with mayonnaise. If you are using home-made mayonnaise add a dessertspoonful of French mustard to the mixture. With bottled mayonnaise or salad cream add French mustard to it until you can really taste it above the other flavours. Add thick cream to make the mixture smoother for special occasions!

Celeriac Soup

Celeriac
Milk
Boiled potato
Salt and pepper
Butter
Cream
Chicken stock
Parsley

Clean (but do not peel) and cut up the celeriac and boil it until it is soft. Then remove the peel. Make a purée of the flesh. Mix it with an equal weight of boiled potatoes and 1 pint of chicken stock. Add a knob of butter and salt and pepper if necessary, and some cream or top of the milk. Adjust the consistency of the soup with more milk, bring it to the boil, and serve with chopped parsley and croûtons.

The vegetable purée, without the chicken stock or milk, is good with meat dishes instead of potato by itself.

CHICORY

Chicory looks like an elongated smooth lettuce heart, white with green tips. Chopped into rings it can be served as salad, alone, or combined with other salad ingredients, with any dressing you like, instead of lettuce. It tastes rather more bitter than lettuce.

Because chicory stays in one piece, as long as it is not boiled too vigorously, it also cooks well. It can also be bought tinned.

Ham and Chicory in Cheese Sauce

Chicory hearts
Slices of ham
Plain flour
Chicken stock or Béchamel
sauce (see page 140)
Grated cheese

Put the chicory in a heavy saucepan in just enough chicken stock to cover it, for 10 minutes. Then wrap a slice of ham round each piece of chicory and pack them into a fireproof dish. Make a roux with the flour and butter, and add the stock in which the chicory was cooked, until the sauce is the consistency of cream. Then put grated cheese on top, and cook, uncovered, until it is golden. If you don't like cheese, leave it out and sprinkle the top with breadcrumbs instead.

Or split the chicory and wrap ham slices round each piece. Lay them in a fireproof dish and dot generously with knobs of butter. Make some thin Béchamel sauce and pour it over the chicory. Bake this in a medium oven for ½ hour, and then sprinkle cheese or breadcrumbs on top, and brown off under the grill.

COURGETTES (ZUCCHINI)

These are small green marrows, which have a variety of names but are usually called courgettes in this country. They have a delicate taste and, by themselves or combined with other vegetables, go well with steak, all kinds of grilled or fried meat, sausages or bacon.

Like aubergines, courgettes should, if the recipe demands that they be sliced, be cut up an hour before use and put in a colander with plenty of salt sprinkled over them, to take out the liquid and with it a slight bitterness. The skin is usually eaten, and unless the courgettes are getting a bit old or are very dirty, there is no point in removing it.

Courgettes Agrodolce

½ lb courgettes
Olive oil
2 tbspn wine vinegar
Saltspoonful cinnamon
1 heaped tbspn sugar
Salt and pepper

Cut the courgettes into quarter-inch slices and salt them. After an hour drain and dry the slices. Heat 2 tablespoonsful of olive oil in a heavy pan and sauté the courgettes until they are changing colour to golden, and becoming soft. When they are soft add the vinegar, sugar and cinnamon. Continue cooking until the liquid has reduced to a light syrup (be careful not to burn the food, which can happen very easily once the sugar has been added). Serve as an accompaniment to any grilled or fried meat.

Courgette Fritters

Courgettes
Thick frying batter
  (see page 140)
Avgolemno sauce (see page 139)
  or Garlic sauce (see page 147)
Olive oil

Slice and salt the courgettes. After an hour dry them and dip them in batter and fry them in hot oil. They are excellent served just like this as a vegetable, but even better with avgolemno or garlic sauce.

Courgettes Provençale

1 lb courgettes
½ lb rice
1 lb skinned tomatoes
  or tin tomatoes
1 pt chicken stock
1 large onion
Grated cheese
3 unskinned tomatoes
Parsley
2 cloves chopped garlic
Plain flour
Salt and pepper

Prepare and cook the courgettes as for Courgettes Agrodolce, but dip the pieces in flour before sautéing them. Cook the rice in chicken stock, and cook the skinned tomatoes and onion, garlic and parsley in a heavy pan in oil, until they are just soft.

    Butter a deep fireproof dish and put in alternative layers of courgettes, rice, and tomato and onion mixture. Top off the dish with a layer of uncooked sliced tomatoes, and cover them with grated cheese. Bake in a medium oven until the cheese is browned.

Mint Courgettes

½ lb courgettes
1 tbspn chopped mint fresh or
  dried
Salt and pepper
Olive oil

Prepare and cook the courgettes as above. Sprinkle the mint

into the vegetables and allow them to cook a few minutes long. Then drain off surplus oil, and season to taste. Serve as a vegetable with meat dishes.

Ratatouille

2 big courgettes	1 small green pepper
1 large aubergine	1 small red pepper
1 large onion	6 coriander seeds
1 clove garlic	1 dssrtspn dried basil
½ lb or small tin tomatoes	

Slice the courgettes and aubergines and salt them. After an hour drain and dry, and sauté them in oil until soft but not mushy. Put them aside while you sauté the onions in the same oil (add a little more if necessary). Then add the tomatoes and garlic, the cooked aubergines and courgettes, add the herbs and season to taste. Cook for a few minutes longer to blend the ingredients together.

This can be served as a vegetable with grills or with sausages, as it is. Or put the ratatouille in a fireproof dish and lay chippolata sausages, which have been lightly precooked, on the top, cover with grated cheese and put in a medium oven until the sausages and cheese are brown.

Salad Courgettes

Slice and salt the courgettes. After an hour dry them and boil the slices until tender, but not mushy. Drain, and when cold cover with vinaigrette dressing.

KOHLRABI

The stem of this plant swells above ground to form a fleshy ball. It has a sickly turnip-like flavour and should be cooked exactly as you would a turnip. Or boil it in salted water till soft, drain, and serve with Béchamel sauce (see page 140), garnished with chopped chives or parsley. The recipes given on page 62 for Celeriac and also suitable for kohlrabi.

MUSHROOMS AND OTHER FUNGI

Mushrooms, boletus, chanterelles and a few other edible fungi can be bought dried or in tins. Their best use is as flavouring for meat dishes where a recipe calls especially for them. All grocers sell fresh cultivated mushrooms nowadays, but dried or tinned mushrooms are useful in the store cupboard as a standby. Other fungi are unobtainable in this country except in tins, and others, although they do grow wild here, can be tricky to identify, so are safer bought out of tins or jars. See also 'Truffles'.

OKRA or BAHMI

Green vegetables about four or five inches long, they are fluted pods containing seeds. Known also as ladies fingers or gumbo, they can be bought fresh or tinned. Drain and rinse before use. They are an extremely pleasant sweet green vegetable eaten by themselves or mixed with others in the same way as courgettes and aubergines.

Dried okra can be bought, but must be steeped in water to swell it before use, and then drained and rinsed.

Okra and Chicken Salad

1 tin or ½ lb okra	Lemon juice
Sliced cooked chicken	Cayenne pepper
1 lb thinly sliced tomatoes	Tarragon vinegar
2 chopped shallots	Watercress
Olive oil	

Boil the whole okra for 10 minutes in salted water. Drain and dry. If you are using tinned okra, no boiling is needed. Put the okra in the bottom of a bowl, and put thin slices of chicken on it. Then add a layer of tomatoes and shallot, then more chicken and tomatoes until the bowl is nearly full. Sprinkle lemon juice, olive oil and cayenne pepper on the top layer of tomato, and put on a thick layer of watercress which has already been dressed with a vinaigrette dressing made from olive oil and tarragon vinegar and salt.

An easily made, but slightly different salad.

Okra in Tomato Sauce

½ lb okra, or 1 tin	Olive oil
1 onion	Clove garlic
4 tomatoes	Salt and pepper

Chop the onion and sauté it until golden in the oil. Blanch the okra as above and add it to the onion and continue cooking until it is just browning. Then add the chopped tomatoes and crushed garlic, put a lid on the pan and let it cook slowly for ½ hour. Remove the lid, season to taste and stir well, and cook fast for another 5 minutes before serving. The juices from the tomato should be thick and not watery.

Sautéed Okra

Take the stems from each pod, and drop them into boiling water to blanch for a few minutes. Drain them dry, and fry them in butter. Cook the vegetables slowly for about 10 minutes until soft and just beginning to colour. They are excellent as a vegetable with any grilled meat, or with omelette.

OLIVES

Sold in jars and loose, olives come in various types. Black olives are gathered when ripe and put into boiling brine before being dried and pickled in oil. Green olives are picked unripe and treated with a hot alkali solution before being pickled in spiced brine. They can be bought unstoned, or stoned and stuffed with pieces of anchovy or red pepper or nuts. Black olives are much blander and not so salty as green olives. Both are excellent as appetisers, as hors d'oeuvre, or salad ingredients. Many recipes for hot beef dishes include olives, which are rather neglected here for general cooking. They are of course the source of olive oil (see page 145).

Beef Stew with Olives

1 lb good stewing steak	Bouquet garni
1 rasher belly pork	Olive oil
2 onions	Salt and pepper
2 carrots	¼ pint red wine
2 tomatoes	12 stoned black olives
Beef stock	2 oz mushrooms
Little rum or brandy	Plain flour
1 clove garlic	

Cut the meat into pieces. Put the pork pieces into a heavy pan with just a little oil and fry them until they are crisp. Transfer them to a casserole. Dip the beef into seasoned flour and sauté it in the pork fat and oil, adding more oil if necessary, until lightly browned. While it is cooking add the crushed garlic. Remove it to the casserole. Put in the sliced carrots, onions and bouquet garni, and the wine, and enough beef stock to cover, and cook, covered, in a low oven for 1½ hours. Take the casserole out of the oven, add the stoned olives and the mushrooms, which should have been lightly sautéed in oil. Put the casserole back in the oven and continue cooking for another half hour. Just before serving, stir in a tablespoonful of rum or brandy.

Using the same ingredients, but omitting the flour and the beef stock, put them in layers in a casserole. First some olive oil, then the pork pieces and the carrots and onions. Cut the beef into slices, not chunks, and pack these in next. Put the garlic cut into little slivers, and the bouquet garni, on to the meat, and sprinkle a little more oil on top. Put the covered casserole into a moderate oven for ½ hour, by which time it should be bubbling, and pour the wine over the meat. Cover the casserole tightly with foil and its own lid, and turn the oven right down. Cook for 3 hours, but check once or twice after 2 hours to see that it has not got too dry. Add a little more wine if necessary. After 2 hours, add the stoned olives and the sautéed mushrooms.

Pour off the gravy and skim off any surplus fat. Then put the gravy back over the stew, piled in a deep serving dish.

Sautéed Rabbit with Olives

1 rabbit	Wineglass sherry
Pepper and salt	1 beef stock cube
Olive oil	¼ lb green olives
2 onions	Bunch of thyme, bay, parsley,
6 anchovy fillets	tarragon and chervil

Joint the rabbit and season it with salt and pepper. Sauté it in a heavy pan in olive oil, with the sliced onions. Add the anchovies and the sherry when the meat and onions are golden, and after 5 minutes add a pint of beef stock. Make the herbs into a bunch and hang them in the stew. Let it simmer for an hour, skimming it frequently. Then remove the meat and herbs, and put the sauce through a blender, so that it is a thick gravy.

Put the rabbit back in the sauce and bring it to the boil.

Meanwhile the olives should be put in a small covered dish, in the oven with a little oil, and braised without being allowed to overcook, shrivel or burn.

Make a border of creamed potatoes or croûtons of fried bread around a serving dish and pile the rabbit in its sauce in the middle. Garnish with the braised olives and sprinkle with a little chopped chervil and tarragon.

These two recipes really illustrate differing methods of cooking meat in a casserole, and one can add other ingredients to provide different flavours, such as pieces of green pepper, a few anchovies, parsnips, chopped gherkins. Or add colour and another flavour with a dessertspoonful of paprika. Or liven it up with a small piece of fresh chilli or a pinch of chilli powder. Or use beer instead of wine to moisten the dish to make the gravy. It is the inclusion of the olives and the use of olive oil for cooking which give the stews their Mediterranean type taste.

To Keep Olives

Green olives bought loose by the pound usually get eaten up very quickly, but you may wish to keep some for future use. As soon as you get them home, dry them gently in a clean cloth. Prick each olive with a fork or slit it, and put them in clean jars with cut garlic, a few stalks of thyme, tarragon or oregano and a tablespoonful of sherry and vinegar mixed. Fill up the jars with olive oil. As the olives are eaten the oil can be used for cooking or to preserve another batch of olives.

PALM HEARTS

These can be bought in tins and are a very good salad ingredient, cut in half and dressed with any vinaigrette dressing. Heated in their own juice they are an excellent light vegetable with a slightly asparagus-like flavour, which goes well with chicken or with egg dishes. Or they can be served hot with Hollandaise sauce (see page 141), sprinkled with a little cheese, as a light supper dish.

Chinese Palm Hearts and Bean Sprout Salad

Palm hearts	Vinegar
Canned bean sprouts	Brown sugar
Crisp lettuce	Water chestnuts
Spring onions	Salt and pepper
Prawns	

Drain and slice the palm hearts thinly, drain and add the bean sprouts, and drain and slice and add the water chestnuts, if you wish to include them. Make a bed of crisp shredded lettuce and chopped spring onion, with the palm heart mixture in the middle.

Drain the prawns and dust them with a little cayenne pepper, and add them to the pile as prettily as possible.

Sweeten a little vinegar with brown sugar, add salt, and sprinkle the whole dish with this dressing.

Chill before serving, as this salad *must* be crisp.

PEPPERS, GREEN AND RED

Once a rarity in this country, peppers are now on sale in almost every greengrocers. The flesh of the fresh green pepper is crisp and hard and juicy with its own special flavour, and cut into strips is marvellous in mixed salad, or by itself with fresh bread, good butter and fine cheese.

The riper red peppers are not quite so crisp, slightly sweet, but many prefer their rather blander taste. Pepper can be added to almost anything, rather as one uses onions, and goes with any stewed meat dish. Peppers can be stuffed with all kinds of meat and rice mixtures, or used as a basis for a variety of dishes in such proportion that the predominant flavour is that of the pepper. Tinned peppers may be substituted for fresh in any cooked dish, except that fresh peppers are better for stuffing because they are firmer.

Pepper Sauce

2 tbspn wine vinegar	1 dssrtspn English mustard
½ pint beef stock	1 dssrtspn French mustard
2 sliced tomatoes	1 tspn chutney
Pinch cayenne pepper	1 tspn sugar
3 red peppers	

Remove the seeds from the peppers and put them with the vinegar, stock, tomatoes, cayenne, mustards, chutney and sugar, and boil them all together for ¼ hour. Then sieve the mixture or put it through an electric blender. Chop the peppers small and put them into the sauce and bring it back to the boil.

An unusual sauce with grilled steak, or grilled veal, or roast leg of lamb.

Pepper Turkey

1 lb cold turkey	Salt and pepper
2 green peppers	1 cup top of the milk
2 tbspn salad cream	¼ pint thick cream
Wineglassful sweet sherry	4 oz mushrooms
Butter	Pinch nutmeg
2 tbspn plain flour	

Make a roux with 3 tablespoonsful butter and flour, add salt and nutmeg, and stir in the top of milk until you have a thick sauce. Add the salad cream and cream, and blend the sauce well. Add the diced turkey.

Sauté the sliced pepper and mushrooms in butter until tender, and add them to the sauce. Blend in the sherry, and serve with plain boiled rice.

This is a very good way of serving some of the Christmas cold turkey and the rich and piquant flavour makes it a great favourite with my family.

Piperade

1 lb onions	Salt and pepper
1 lb tomatoes, or tin	6 eggs
2 large red peppers	Olive oil

Slice the onions and cook them in the oil, in a heavy pan, until they are golden, then add the peppers and, when they too are soft, add the tomatoes. Cook the whole lot slowly, stirring it up together until it is thick purée. Season it to taste, and then add the beaten eggs and keep stirring. It should turn into a kind of scrambled egg. It is important not to overcook the mixture once the egg is added, for if the egg goes too hard the dish is spoiled. Piperade goes very well with fried or grilled bacon or sausages.

The same mixture, with the addition of a crushed clove of garlic, and with the egg left out, makes a good vegetable dish to eat with any grilled meat.

Stuffed Peppers

6 good shaped green peppers
½ lb minced beef, veal, or 6 oz minced chicken and 2 oz minced ham, or small tin of tuna fish
2 oz rice
1 clove garlic

1 small onion
Chicken stock
2 tbspn white wine or wine vinegar
1 tbspn sugar
1 small tin tomato purée

Cut the tops off the peppers and take out the seeds. Mix together the meat, rice, chopped onion, and garlic, and season with salt and pepper. Half fill the cavities in the peppers. Replace the tops and pack the peppers into a saucepan so that they cannot fall over, and the tops do not slide off. Mix the tomato purée and sugar with enough chicken stock just to cover the peppers. Cover the saucepan, bring the contents to the boil, and then simmer very slowly until the peppers are tender and most of the liquid has been absorbed, which will take about 1 hour. Serve hot or cold.

To Skin Peppers

To make peppers easy to skin, if it is only the flesh you wish to use, put them under a grill and turn them several times, cooking until all the surface is slightly charred. The skin will then come off easily under cold running water.

SALISFY OR OYSTER PLANT

This root can be bought fresh or in tins. True salisfy is white skinned, but the dark skinned variety (scorzonera) tastes almost the same.

Because it discolours on exposure to air, the roots should be put into water with a little lemon juice or vinegar in it immediately they are scraped or peeled. Cut the roots into pieces and boil them in salted water with a little lemon juice in it for about half an hour or until tender. Serve hot with plenty of melted butter, or in Béchamel sauce (see page 140), or allow to cool and season with vinaigrette dressing (see page 147), garnish with parsley, chervil or tarragon, and serve as a salad.

Tinned salisfy only needs heating or dressing before use, or use straight out of the tin to make fritters.

Salisfy Fritters

Cook the salisfy as above. Put the cut pieces into a deep dish, season with salt and pepper, a little lemon juice and some chopped parsley, and leave them for ½ hour to absorb flavour. Dip the pieces in light batter (see page 140) and cook in deep fat. Or dip the pieces in milk and roll them in bread crumbs and sauté them in a frying pan until golden.

SAUERKRAUT

Pickled white cabbage is perhaps the commonest vegetable in Europe, especially in parts of Germany and Austria, and also the Balkans. It is not all that popular here, although it does go very well indeed with some meat dishes. It is sold in tins, but it is not good enough just to heat up the contents and serve it straight as a vegetable, just rather sharp acid cabbage. It must be properly cooked to be interesting and appetising.

Sauerkraut

1 large tin sauerkraut, drained	Bayleaf
1 sweet apple	Clove of garlic
1 chopped onion	1 tspn caraway seed (if liked)
10 juniper berries	Glass white wine
Salt and pepper to taste	Butter

Put all the ingredients except the butter and wine together in a saucepan with enough water to prevent burning, cover and cook slowly for ½ hour, stirring frequently. Then pour the wine, and the butter which should be melted and just brown, over the sauerkraut, and serve it at once. Serve sauerkraut with hot gammon steaks, Frankfurters and pork.

Sauerkraut and Hock

Sauerkraut cooked as above	1 grated potato
1 large hock	1 pint water

Put the hock and the water in a heavy saucepan or casserole and simmer it slowly on top of the stove for 1½ hours. Then put the sauerkraut carefully in the liquid under the hock, and let it all simmer very slowly for another hour. Then if the liquor is watery, add the grated potato to thicken it, and bring it all to the boil once again.

Sauerkraut Salad

1 tin sauerkraut	Sugar
3 tbspn olive oil	Mayonnaise or tomato dressing
Salt	(see page 143)

Squeeze all the liquid out of the sauerkraut, and put it in a bowl with plenty of dressing, stir it well with a fork until the dressing is spread throughout.

SQUASH OR PUMPKINS

All the marrows and pumpkins can be called squashes, and there are dozens of varieties. In America they are divided into summer and winter squashes. The summer squashes being courgettes, marrows and other thin skinned tender seeded varieties. Winter squashes come ripe in the autumn and are tougher skinned with harder seeds. What we usually call pumpkins—the big yellow gourds with yellow flesh—are the type most likely to be on sale here. Squashes are so mild in flavour that they are barely worth eating without a bit of dressing up, but they do make a good base vegetable, and absorb and carry flavours well. Because they are much more common here, courgettes have been treated under their own heading, but the recipes given for them may also be used for cooking pumpkin or marrow.

Colache

2 lb pumpkin	2 oz butter
1 tin sweet corn or 4 corn cobs	1 small onion
3 ripe tomatoes, or 1 small tin	Salt and pepper

Remove the rind of the pumpkin unless it is very tender, and discard the pips if they are hard. Dice it. Cut up the skinned tomatoes. Cook the sliced onion in the butter until it is soft, and add all the other ingredients. Cook covered over a low heat for ½ hour, stirring to prevent burning. All the ingredients should be cooked but not mushy. Season to taste and serve with fried chippolata sausages or grilled bacon.

Honey-Baked Squash

2 medium sized acorn squash
Melted butter
4 dssrtspn honey
1 lb cooked chippolata sausages

Cut the squash in half lengthwise, remove the seeds and bake them uncovered but cut side down in a medium oven for about 40 minutes. Turn them the other way up, brush the insides with butter and pour in a spoonful of honey in each piece. Divide the sausages equally into each squash, and bake for a further 20 minutes.

Pumpkin Pie

½ pint pumpkin purée
2 eggs
½ pint milk
3 oz sugar
1 tbspn rum
Pinch grated nutmeg, cinnamon, ginger and ground cloves, or
1 tspn crushed aniseed
Shortcrust pastry

Stew the peeled and seeded pumpkin, in just enough water to prevent it from burning, until it is tender enough to put through a blender. Add the other ingredients to the ½ pint purée with the beaten eggs. Line a pie dish with the pastry and fill it with the pumpkin mixture. Bake in a hot oven at 450 (gas 8) for 15 minutes, then turn down the heat and finish cooking at 350 (gas 4) for another 20 minutes.

Roast Pumpkin

Peel the pumpkin, cut it into fairly large chunks, and roast it round the meat in hot dripping, just as one does potatoes.

Sweet Winter Squash

1 pumpkin
To each ½ lb flesh allow:
  1 tbspn butter
  1 tspn moist brown sugar
  1 tbspn rum
  pinch salt
pinch ginger
Orange juice
Mixed nuts and raisins
Cream

Bake the pumpkin whole in the oven at 375 deg. (gas 5) for 1½ hours. When it feels soft (test with a skewer), take it out, cut it in half and remove the seeds. Then peel the pumpkin and mash the flesh thoroughly with the butter, rum, sugar, salt and ginger. Mix in enough orange juice to make it the consistency of thick cream. Chill it well, sprinkle it with mixed nuts and raisins, and serve with plenty of cream.

SUCCOTASH

This is a vegetable mixture which is basically sweet corn and lima beans, and is used as an accompaniment to meat dishes. It can be bought in tins.

SWEET CORN

Although sweet corn, fresh, tinned and frozen, has been on the market for years, and although it is just about the commonest vegetable there is in America, many people are still not quite sure of its best uses. Oddly enough, although it is excellent food and extremely tasty, it is looked upon in much of Europe as fit only for animals, and this probably accounts for the fact that it is not a 'traditional' food here. Also it is only comparatively recently that strains of corn which can be relied upon to ripen in Britain and in Northern Europe have been developed for eating.

When buying corn fresh and still on the cob, with its green husk round it, it is necessary to check whether it is fit to eat. The silk at the top of the cob should be brown and going wrinkled, but is almost impossible to tell whether or not the cob beneath is full and ripe. Retailers do not like to part the husk to allow you to inspect the cobs, because they dry very quickly. A helpful retailer will cut out a small square of husk with a sharp knife, like a little window, through which you can see the corn. It should be bright pale yellow, neither pale green nor light orange, and the grain should be full and shiny, not wrinkled.

Cooking Sweet Corn

Strip the husk and silk from the cobs and cut off the stalks. Put them in a saucepan containing just enough water, or half milk and half water, to cover the corn. Add a tablespoonful of sugar and boil for from 5 to 10 minutes, no longer, according to the maturity of the cobs. Longer boiling will not soften overripe cobs, in fact it seems to make them harder. Drain the cobs and serve on a hot plate with plenty of butter, salt and black pepper. Frozen cobs can be cooked in the same way.

Or prepare as above, and spread each cob with butter, salt and pepper. Wrap each cob in baking foil and cook it for 20 minutes in an oven at 400 deg. or gas 6. Use only young cobs, or frozen cobs.

Alternatively, spread butter all over the cobs and grill them, turning them round as they brown, until cooked on all sides.

Tinned whole kernel sweet corn is excellent as vegetable with other dishes, and only needs heating up with butter.

Cream style corn, as it is called when the kernels are tinned in their own juice, is excellent for making fritters to accompany any bacon or sausage or other fried or grilled food.

Sweet Corn Fritters

1 can cream style sweet corn
2 tbspn S.R. flour
1 egg

Additions:
fried onion rings or chopped green peppers, or crumbled cooked bacon, or minced ham

Empty the corn into a bowl and stir in the flour and the beaten egg. Add extra ingredients if liked.

The mixture should be a thick batter. Drop a big tablespoonful of it into very hot deep oil in a heavy frying pan, and cook on both sides. The outsides should be crisp and brown, and the insides just set and spongy, but not still runny.

SWEET POTATO

These are also known as yams, and are large fleshy tubers which can be cooked exactly like potatoes, in many different ways. There are several varieties varying slightly in colour and shape, but none of them tastes like ordinary potatoes; they are much sweeter, not unlike chestnuts, so are *not* a substitute for ordinary potatoes, but are more often eaten with butter or honey, or sprinkled with sugar or jam. Sliced sweet potatoes can be cooked in a pie with apples. Mashed sweet potatoes with additions do go well with ham.

One variety of small yams can be bought tinned in a sweet syrup.

Baked Sweet Potatoes

Clean the potatoes and bake them in their skins until tender, but do be sure to cut a small piece off one end, or when half cooked, to prick it two or three times with a fork, otherwise it will probably explode inside the oven. Serve with plenty of butter and salt.

Boiled Sweet Potatoes

Boil the cleaned potatoes in their jackets, or pare them and boil them just like ordinary potatoes, but do not salt the water. Mash the potatoes when cooked with butter, a little salt, a little cream or top of the milk, and a little dry sherry to taste. If the mash is not quite sweet enough, beat in some moist brown sugar. Garnish with grated lemon rind and a dusting of cinnamon.

Sweet Potato and Apple Pie

3 medium-sized sweet potatoes	Pinch cinnamon
1 lb sliced cooking apples	Butter
2 oz brown sugar	Wineglassful cider or water

Peel the sweet potatoes and slice them ½ inch thick. Cook them until just tender in a little water. Grease a pie dish and put the potato and apples in the dish in layers, sprinkling each layer with sugar and cinnamon. Dot 3 oz butter over the top and add a wineglassful of cider or water, and bake in a moderate oven for about an hour until the apples are cooked and the top nicely browned.

Sweet Potato Patties

1 lb mashed sweet potato	¼ pint water
2 tbspn S.R. flour	Pinch salt
2 oz butter	1 lemon
2 well beaten eggs	Cinnamon
4 oz brown sugar	1 tbspn sherry

Mix all the ingredients together and beat them until they are light. Half fill greased patty tins with the mixture and bake in a moderate oven for about 35 minutes.

Yam Dumplings

½ lb cooked mashed yams
3 oz melted butter
1 beaten egg

4 oz S.R. flour
½ tspn salt

Combine the first three ingredients then blend in the flour and salt. Divide it and drop it by the tablespoonful into a hot chicken or veal casserole. Cook in a moderate oven for about 35 minutes.

TRUFFLES

'Whoever says "truffles" utters a great word which arouses erotic and gastronomic memories among the skirted sex, and memories gastronomic and erotic among the bearded sex.' Brillat-Savarin.

Tinned truffles and tinned truffle peelings are extremely useful here because natural fresh truffles are not found in this country. Truffles grow underground in association with oaks and hazels and although they can be found (by specially trained dogs or even pigs) in many places on the Continent, black truffles from the district of Perigord are supposed to best the best. They are used for their scent in flavourings and stuffings. White truffles are more often eaten raw or very lightly cooked, for their own taste. Try some thin slices on top of a fondue (see page 126).

There are those who believe the flavour of truffles to be the finest taste there is, others see nothing in it and cannot understand why anyone is prepared to pay the very high prices demanded for truffles.

Any reference to Perigeux on a menu means that the dish referred to contains truffles, as does sauce Perigeux, which is marvellous with ham, steak or poultry or salt pork (see page 145).

Delicatessen Cookery

Quiches and Salmon

Hams

Spices, green and black olives, turkey, pâté en croûte

Pâtés

Bread

Pickles, turkey, quiches

Lichees and raspberries

Strawberries, brie, chicken and rosemary

Olive oil in cans and bottles.
Herbed olive oil. Packet cheeses

Duck Pâté with Truffles

1 duck with its liver
3 oz liver pâté
2 lbs lean pork
½ lb fat pork belly in thin rashers
1 small tin truffles
4 oz brandy
1 egg
Salt and pepper
1 pinch each nutmeg, cloves, cinnamon
1 tspn allspice
Butter

Remove all the duck meat from the carcase and mince it with the pork through a coarse mincer, or chop it finely. Put it into a bowl and pour the brandy over it, add the seasonings and stir it all together. Leave it for at least 2 hours to marinate then blend it all together again with the beaten egg.

Grease a terrine with butter and line it with fat pork slices. Put half the duck and pork mixture in the bottom of the terrine. Mix together the liver pâté, the chopped duck liver and the truffles and put it on top of the first layer. Then fill the terrine with the other half of the duck and pork mixture. Cover the top with fat pork rashers. Put a layer of baking foil on as a lid and then the terrine lid. Cook in a bain marie until the pâté is coming away from the sides of the terrine, for about 1½ to 2 hours in a slow oven. Remove from the oven and the bain marie, take off the foil lid, reverse terrine lid, and use it to press the pâté down gently, being careful not to spill the juices. Put a weight on the lid to hold it down and leave the terrine overnight to cool and set.

Partridge with Truffles

2 partridges
1 small tin truffles
Wineglassful sherry
2 oz chopped bacon
1 beef stock cube
Butter

Truss the partridges for roasting, then smear a little butter on the breasts. Put them into a casserole and add the liquor from the truffles and the sherry. Sprinkle in the chopped bacon. Put on the lid and cook in a medium/hot oven about 400 deg. (gas 6) for about ¾ hour. They should be tender, but not dry. Remove the birds and keep them hot. Add the gravy from the casserole to the stock in a heavy saucepan and cook them together until the gravy is reduced by half. Add the truffles but do not boil again.

Serve the birds on croûtons of fried bread with the sauce poured over them.

Truffled Pork

1 small (¾ oz) tin truffles
4 lb joint of pork
White wine

Salt and pepper
Butter

Bone the joint. Using a very sharp knife, make slits in the fat, big enough to take little slices of the truffles. Use up all the truffles, putting some in the bone cavity as well, but retain the liquid from the tin. Rub a little salt and black pepper on the joint, and roll and tie it if necessary to keep it firm and well shaped. Put the meat in a covered roasting dish with a small knob of butter on top and roast it in a medium oven, for about 1¾ hours. When it is done put the joint on to a serving dish. Remove as much of the pork fat from the juices in the pan as possible. Pour a glass of white wine into the pan and let the gravy boil till it has reduced by half. Then add the juice from the truffle tin and bring the gravy to simmering point again, but do not let it bubble. Season to taste. Serve this gravy very hot with the roast meat, plain boiled potatoes or plain boiled rice, and a green salad.

Truffle Omelette

If you need just a few truffles for a recipe and have to open a tin, make yourself a truffle omelette with the remainder. Or if you are a dab hand at making omelettes and wish to serve something quite special, use a whole tin of truffles.

Cook the omelette in your usual way, but 4 hours before you wish to cook it, break the eggs into a bowl with the drained sliced truffles, and cover with a cloth. Beat up the eggs and truffles with a fork just before cooking.

VINE LEAVES

Vine leaves can occasionally be bought fresh, and most delicatessen stock them in tins ready for use. Stuffed vine leaves or 'dolmades' can also be bought tinned, but are extremely easy to make at home. The leaves of hazel can be used as a substitute, but there is no real substitute for the faintly resinous woody flavour of vine leaves.

Fresh vine leaves wrapped round small fish, partridges, chicken pieces, which are then seasoned and baked in the oven with plenty of butter and perhaps a little wine to moisten them, add something to the flavour of the food.

Dolmades

2 doz vine leaves, fresh or tinned
4 oz rice
½ pint olive oil
1 tspn dill or fennel
2 shallots or equivalent in spring onions
2 tspn chopped fresh mint
Boiling water
Salt and pepper

If the vine leaves are tinned they can be used without further cooking. Fresh vine leaves should be dropped into boiling water and blanched for 3 minutes.

Cook the rice in ½ pint of boiling water for 5 minutes only, then add all the other ingredients (except the vine leaves) and cook the mixture for another 10 minutes until the rice is done, stirring all the time. Season with salt and pepper and leave it to cool for a bit or you will burn your fingers in the next process. Lay a vine leaf on the palm of your left hand, with the stem at your wrist. Put a heaped teaspoonful of the filling in the middle of the leaf. Use more if it is a very big leaf. Then, starting at the stem end, roll the vine leaf over the rice, and turn the ends in to make a little fat envelope. As you make each dolmade, put it into the bottom of a heavy saucepan, packing in until you have a layer. Then make another layer, until the rice is all used up. Just cover the contents of the pan with water, and put a saucer or plate on top of the dolmades so that they remain still while being cooked, and don't break up. Cook very slowly for about ¾ hour. Dolmades made up in tins can be heated by being put with all the oil and liquid from the tin into a heavy saucepan over a very low flame. Keep the lid on and cook for a few minutes until warmed through.

Serve dolmades either hot or cold. Natural yoghurt goes well with cold dolmades, and avgolemno (see page 139) is perfect with hot ones. They make an excellent hot extra with any grilled meat, or an hors d'oeuvre or salad dish.

Or make big plain omelettes and turn them over preheated stuffed vine leaves, 3 to an omelette. This makes an excellent supper dish, or—just one or two in a small omelette—entrée.

Stuffed Vine Leaves in Wine

Vine leaves
1 onion
¼ pint olive oil
6 tbspn rice

4 tspn pine nuts
12 oz minced beef
1 tspn dried mint

Prepare the vine leaves as in the previous recipe. Fry the chopped onion in hot olive oil until it is soft, then add the rice. Continue to fry it, stirring frequently until it is golden, then add the meat and the rest of the ingredients. Cook for another 5 minutes until the beef has changed colour. Then stuff the vine leaves with this mixture exactly as in the last recipe, and cook them in exactly the same way in the wine, topping up with just enough water to cover. By the time the liquid has been absorbed, about 45 minutes, the meal should be ready. Eat hot or cold without sauce.

This is a much more filling dish as it contains meat.

SECTION FIVE

Fruit

Most of the comments at the beginning of the vegetable section also apply to fruit. Let it be said at once that few foreign fruits come anything near our home-grown fruit for flavour. Our native raspberries, strawberries, blackberries, blackcurrants, cherries, plums, apples, pears and gooseberries are superb. Even the citrus fruits we know, oranges, grapefruit, etc., which do not grow here but which are so common as to seem native, are better than the lesser-known citrus fruits which are coming into the shops, with the possible exception of limes—of which we do not make half enough use.

Nevertheless, mangos, paw paws, passion fruit, custard apples, avocados and pomegranates do make a nice change, especially of texture, and are at their best in the winter, when our own fruit is at its worst, so they fill a gap, and also mix quite well in fruit salads, etc., with home-grown and citrus fruits. Use mango or paw paw instead of tinned peaches in a fruit salad, and you will see what I mean.

Most foreign fruit is best eaten fresh, by itself or with other fruit, just chilled, with a little cream or sugar if liked. If you think about it, one only starts cooking home-grown fruit when there is a glut of it. Given a few beautiful strawberries or raspberries, for instance, I eat them fresh with cream and sugar and do not cook them. Nevertheless at times when they are plentiful and not too expensive—and for that 'different' meal—try some of the recipes in this section.

AVOCADO PEARS

These big green pears have thick buttery flesh which tastes slightly nutty. Many people think it is a great delicacy, others find it extremely overrated, especially as it is expensive, although plentiful.

Eat avocado plain, just halved and scooped out with a spoon, or with vinaigrette sauce, or in salads, with citrus fruit, or with various hot or cold sauces. It goes well with crab or lobster meat and many fillings are based on these. Dressings should be tart to counteract the richness of the flesh. Avocado is extremely filling and nourishing, so don't serve too much of it at a time. The flesh turns dark when exposed to air, so don't cut the pears till just before serving, unless you immediately put lemon juice on them. Halve them lengthways.

Avocado Soup

2 pints chicken stock
½ lb avocado pears
Salt and pepper
Wineglass dry white wine
Juice of ½ lemon

Scoop out the avocado flesh and chop it. Put the hot stock, seasonings and avocado flesh into a blender and make it into a purée. Heat the wine and lemon juice together but do not boil them, and add them to the purée. Stir well and serve garnished with a slice of lemon.

Baked Avocado with Crab Meat

2 avocados
1 small tin crab meat
½ pint Béchamel sauce (see page 140)
2 tbspn thick cream
2 tbspn tomato purée
Salt and pepper
Tabasco sauce
Grated cheese
Lemon or lime juice

Cut the pears in half and take out the stones. Dress the surfaces thoroughly with lemon or lime juice. Mix the crab meat with thick Béchamel sauce, cream, tomato purée and the seasonings. Put the pears in a shallow fireproof dish and pile the mixture on to them, finishing off with a sprinkling of cheese. Put a little water in the bottom of the dish, and bake uncovered in a medium oven 325/350 deg. (gas 3/4) until the tops are browned; about 25 minutes.

Citrus Dressing for Avocado

1 oz caster sugar
Pinch paprika
Small clove garlic
Pinch salt
¼ pint olive oil
1 tspn Worcester sauce
2 tbspn wine vinegar
2 tbspn orange juice
1 tbspn lemon juice
1 tbspn grapefruit juice

Put all the ingredients together in a screw topped jar and shake them up well. Leave the jar to stand for ½ hour at least before using the dressing so that the flavours blend. Strain the dressing before use to remove the garlic. Smother the halved pears with this. As it contains citric acid it will stop the fruit from discolouring, so this dish can be made up some time before serving.

Rum and Lime Juice Dressing for Avocado

Use the juice of fresh limes if available, otherwise neat lime juice cordial. To each dessertspoonful of rum, add a teaspoonful of lime juice. Made with cordial the dressing will be sweeter. Pour this over the halved fruit, filling the cavity.

Vinaigrette Dressing for Avocado

Cut and dress the pear just before serving. To one dessertspoonful of olive oil add a pinch of salt, a pinch of black pepper and a few drops of lemon juice to taste, and sprinkle this over the halved pear, filling up the cavity made by removing the stone.

CHINESE GOOSEBERRIES or KIWI FRUIT

Tasting faintly of melon and strawberry, these vitamin C rich fruit are imported here from New Zealand fresh or tinned. They are brown, hairy and about 3 inches long, but when cut the flesh is pale green and looks very appetising. Ripe fruit are just soft to the touch. They are quite pleasant eaten straight, scooped out with a spoon, but are much improved by being served with yoghurt, cream or ice cream, or with a dash of liqueur or brandy. They mix well with other fruit such as strawberries, raspberries and bananas to make a fruit salad.

Chinese Gooseberry Chantilly

3 Chinese gooseberries
2 tbspn Kirsch
Small carton cream

2 tbspn icing sugar
Dessert wafers or biscuits

Peel the fruit and dice it. Sprinkle it with Kirsch and leave it in the fridge for an hour to marinate. Whip the cream until it is buttery and sweeten it with icing sugar. Drain off any liquid from the gooseberries into the cream and mix it well, adding a spot more Kirsch if necessary to make it exactly the right thickness to be heaped into small dishes when you have folded in the gooseberry pieces.

Gooseberry Green Salad

1 gooseberry (per serving) Olive oil
1 small stalk celery Lemon juice
4 burnt almonds or cashew nuts

Peel and dice the fruit and dice the celery. Mix in the nuts and sprinkle with a dressing of equal parts of olive oil and lemon juice.

Chinese gooseberries also go well with ham and mayonnaise, but should not be allowed to touch the meat if you are making up open sandwiches or snacks.

CUSTARD APPLE

Small custard apples appear from time to time in the greengrocers. The fruit has green slightly bumpy skin, and the white flesh is studded with black seeds. It has a light pleasant flavour, and is best eaten just as it is scooped out of the rind with a spoon. Spit out the pips.

GUAVA

Guavas can be bought in tins, with or without their seeds. They are usually eaten straight out of the tin with cream, either by themselves or in fruit salad. The fresh fruit, rarely obtainable here, can be made into jam or jelly using standard recipes, or peel and slice the fresh fruit, sprinkle it with sugar, and serve it with cream.

KUMQUAT

These are small elongated oranges which sometimes appear fresh in our shops, and can also be bought tinned. They are usually eaten raw, just like oranges, and can be used to make marmalade, sauces, etc., in exactly the same way as oranges.

Kumquat Salad

A sweet-sour salad which is delicious by itself or good with cold meats and continental sausages for a special meal.

3 tbspn sweet sherry
1 small tin kumquats
1 small tin pineapple
1 pomegranate
1 lemon

4 oz cream cheese
Pinch dry mustard
1 tbspn caster sugar
½ pint cream
Lettuce

Dice the pineapple, and take the seeds out of the kumquats, and slice them thinly. Take the pips out of the pomegranate and put them with the pineapple and kumquat. Pour the sherry over them and leave them to marinate.

Mix together the cream cheese, lemon juice, syrup from the tin of kumquats and the salt, mustard and sugar. Whip the cream until it is very stiff and then fold in the fruit and wine and cheese mixture. Put it in trays in the freezing compartment of the fridge, until it is firm enough to cut but not solid. Arrange pieces of the salad on crisp lettuce, and garnish with a few pineapple chunks and lemon slices.

Whole Preserved Kumquats

1 lb or 1 tin kumquats
½ pint water if fresh fruit is being used

8 oz sugar
¼ pint honey

Wash the fruit and make a small cut in the top of each one. If you are using tinned fruit retain the liquid and prick the fruit with a fork. Bring the water, sugar and honey, or the tin liquid, sugar and honey, to the boil. Put in the fruit and continue boiling over a low flame until the fruit is almost transparent. The liquor should be very thick and syrupy. Be careful not to burn this sugar liquor while boiling. Put the fruit into jars in their syrup and serve as a treat at Christmas time.

LICHEES

Lichees are obtainable both fresh and tinned, although the 'fresh lichees' have in fact been allowed to dry in their shells, which have turned brownish black. Freshly picked ripe lichees are red, a little bigger than cherries. The thin skin is hard and scaly and comes away easily from the white fruit. The skinned fruit are imported canned in syrup, and should be eaten without further cooking. Fresh lichees can be eaten straight, or else put in a syrup made from 4 oz sugar and ½ pint water. Do not cook the lichees, but just leave them to soak in this syrup for about an hour before serving.

LIMES

Fresh limes look like small lemons and are even sharper, but the juice when sweetened has a flavour quite its own, so limes are a most useful citrus fruit. Boiled rice for curry is improved by having lime juice sprinkled on it just before serving. Use 1 lime per lb of rice. A dessertspoonful of lime juice added to the curry itself just before cooking is finished brings out flavour. Lime acts in the same way as lemon to stop other fruits such as apples from going brown. So use lime instead of lemon for any purpose to get an even sharper and slightly different taste.

Lime and Apple Sambal

Equal amounts of lime juice and olive oil

Sweet apples

To make a sweet-sour side dish for curry, peel and core the apples, and slice them. Beat the lime juice and oil together to make enough dressing to coat the fruit.

Lime and Sesame Meringue

2 limes
4 oz brown moist sugar
2 oz roasted sesame seed
2 oz butter

4 eggs
Pinch saffron
2 drops almond essence

Cream together the butter and sugar and add the juice of the limes and the beaten yolks of the eggs. Mix well together and add the saffron, almond essence and sesame seeds. The sesame seeds are roasted by being put in a saucer or shallow tin in a hot oven until they change colour.

Put this mixture into a double saucepan and heat it over boiling water until it thickens, stirring all the time. Do not let it boil. Remove from the heat and spoon the mixture into a shallow baking dish, fold in the stiffly beaten egg whites, and cook for about 20 minutes in a slow oven. Serve hot.

Lime Curd

6 limes	¼ lb unsalted butter
5 eggs	1 lb white sugar

Wash the limes and grate the rind very carefully without taking any of the white pith. Squeeze the juice in with the peel and get rid of any pips. Beat the eggs and put them together with the rind and juice, the butter and the sugar, into a double saucepan. Cook, stirring all the time, until the curd thickens, but do not let it boil. Strain it into pots and cover it straight away.

This curd will not keep very long, but it is so delicious that it will not need to!

Lime Marmalade

To every 12 limes use 1½ lb sugar and 2 pints of water. Peel off the yellow rinds and shred them finely. Squeeze the juice into a heavy saucepan with the sugar and water. Discard the white pith, but put the flesh and pips into a muslin bag tied at the top and suspend it in the liquid. Bring to the boil, stirring frequently and continue cooking until setting point is reached (220 deg.). Lift out the muslin bag and squeeze it over the marmalade so that no jelly is wasted. Let the marmalade cool right down before giving it a last stir and putting it into jars. If the marmalade is bottled while it is still very hot, all the shreds will rise to the top of the jars.

Lemons can be substituted for the limes at the rate of 1 lemon to 2 limes.

Lime Meringue Pie

Pastry case	4 limes
3 eggs	Caster sugar
1 tin condensed milk	Lime juice cordial

Squeeze all the juice from the limes into a cup. Beat together the egg yolks and the condensed milk. Then add the lime juice and beat it in. Taste the mixture and if it is too sharp, beat in some sugar until it seems right to your taste, although this should be unnecessary as the condensed milk is very sweet. Pour the filling into the cooked pastry case. Then beat the egg whites until they are so stiff you can turn the bowl upside down, and add a little sugar, beating that in well. Spread this mixture over the filling, pulling it up into peaks with a fork. Cook for 5 minutes in a moderate to hot oven 400-425 deg. (gas 6/7). Serve cold with whipped cream and/or ice cream, and just a sprinkling of lime juice cordial straight from the bottle.

Lime Pickle (Hot)

12 whole limes
Juice of 3 lemons
4 oz green ginger (see page 160)
2 oz green chillies
2 tbspn salt
2 bay leaves
2 tspn cayenne pepper

Peel and slice the ginger. Remove the seeds from the chillies. Wash and dry the limes and cut them into slices and remove the pips.

Put a layer of lime slices in the bottom of a jar, sprinkle with salt and crushed bay leaf, add some of the chopped chillies and strips of ginger. Repeat these layers until the ingredients are used up and then pour in the lemon juice. Having tied a piece of cloth over the jar, shake it thoroughly but carefully and put it on a windowsill in the sunshine. Each day for 4 days add some more salt and shake the jar again. Remove the cloth and put on a glass or plastic top (never a metal one). Then leave the pickle to mature for a fortnight.

This makes a strong sharp pickle, not for over-sensitive palates. To make it even stronger, put in more cayenne pepper, and leave the seeds in the chillies. To make it less strong, halve the amount of chillies and omit the cayenne pepper.

This is really a basic recipe which can be added to or subtracted from as you wish. It can be made with half limes and half lemons, or lime juice may be substituted for the lemon juice. At a pinch it can be made entirely with lemons and just the juice from half a dozen limes, or tinned natural lime juice, if you can get it.

Spiced Lime Pickle

This very hot pickle is usually served in Indian restaurants with curry and can be bought ready made up in jars, but is well worth making up for yourself.

10 limes	2 tspn fenugreek
5 lemons	1 tbspn cumin seeds
2 tbspn dried chillies	1½ pints olive oil
1 dssrtspn ground black pepper	3 tbspn salt
6 cloves crushed garlic	1 tbspn brown sugar
2 tbspn mustard seed	

Wash and dry the limes and lemons and cut them into pieces removing all the pips. Shake the mustard seed and fenugreek in a dry frying pan over a good flame to roast them for a minute or two, and then grind them down finely. Grind the cumin seed or crush it, but not too fine. Put together the salt, garlic, ginger, mustard and fenugreek, and sprinkle them all over the fruit, stirring well. Then pack the fruit into a jar, adding in the rest of the ingredients in layers so that they are well spread through the pickle. Heat the oil until it is smoking, and keep it hot for 5 minutes, but do not burn it. Let the oil cool so that it will not break the jar, and pour it over the pickle. Leave it loosely covered for a week, then screw down the lid and keep it for another week before using it.

To make a milder pickle cut down on the chillies, or leave them out altogether and substitute a pinch of chilli powder or cayenne pepper.

LINGON BERRIES

Red berries, very like cranberries, used in Scandinavian cooking. They can be bought tinned in this country and used in exactly the same way as cranberries. They make a good filler for thick pancakes.

LOQUATS or JAPANESE MEDLAR

Sweet, slightly tart and refreshing fruit, best eaten straight out of the tin or fresh, if you can get them.

MANGO

A Far-Eastern fruit, about the size of a big pear with green skin which turns yellow as the fruit ripens. The flesh is bright orange, soft, close textured and sweet. Mangos can be eaten raw. Chill the fruit or it may have a slight taste of turpentine. If you serve the fruit whole, then you must provide a very sharp knife as it is quite difficult to cut the flesh away from its very big kernel. In fact it is easier to peel the fruit and cut the flesh away from the kernel in neat slices, and put it into plates or glasses, before serving with cream or ice cream.

Mango and Rice Pudding

1 lb rice	Saffron
4 mangos	¼ pint milk
Sugar	¼ pint cream

Skin the mangos and remove the flesh from the kernel, put it in an electric blender and make it into a purée. Boil the milk and whip the cream until it is very thick. Then blend this with the mango purée. Add the saffron, and sugar to taste. The aim is to make a thick creamy mango purée, the consistency of which can be adjusted by adding more or less boiled milk.

Meanwhile boil the rice until it is really soft. Drain it and put a layer in a deep, well buttered fireproof dish. Add a layer of half the mango cream, and another layer of rice, then the rest of the mango cream, and finish with another layer of rice. Put several knobs of butter on top and bake in a slow oven until the top is slightly browned. It should be well set by this time, and ready to serve hot or cold with a jug of single cream.

Mango Chutney

The most famous and best of chutneys to serve with curry, it is easy to make, but the fruit must be green, not ripe, or it will go mushy.

1 lb green mangos	1 oz mustard seed or dry mustard
1 oz dry chillies	¼ lb sultanas
3 cloves garlic	1 tsbn turmeric
½ pint wine vinegar	Salt
1 lb brown moist sugar	
2 oz root ginger	

Peel the mangos and cut the flesh from the stones, slice it into pieces and put them in a colander. Sprinkle with salt and leave overnight to drain.

Chop, crush and pound the chillies and garlic in a little of the vinegar. Then put all the ingredients except the mangos into a saucepan and boil together until the liquid turns to thick syrup —be careful it does not burn. Then add the mangos and continue to cook slowly until the pieces are tender but not mushy. Put the pickle into jars and seal them. This should keep well.

Mango Fool

6 mangos or 1 tin	Small carton double cream
Sugar to taste	Chopped nuts

Peel the fresh mangos and cut all the flesh from the stones. Put the flesh into a pan with just enough water to stop it burning and cook until it is tender. Put through a sieve or blender and when cool add the sugar and whipped cream. Decorate with nuts.

If tinned mangos are used, do not cook them.

NECTARINE

Nectarines are a smooth-skinned peach, and can be eaten fresh or cooked by any recipe for peaches.

PASSION FRUIT or GRANADILLAS

These are small round purplish-brown fruit which do not look particularly appetising. However, when cut in half they reveal bright yellow, green and pink interiors. They have a delightful sweet-sour flavour, of which the sour element is rather like fresh limes. Most refreshing small delicacies, if a little pippy (eat the pips).

Serve cut in half on a bed of crushed ice in small bowls, and provide a small teaspoon with which to scoop out the flesh. They are excellent before or after a rich meal.

Tinned passion fruit pulp blends well into fruit cream and jellies.

PAW PAWS or PAPAYA

The paw paws offered for sale in this country are small compared to those which can be bought in countries where they grow. The texture is creamy and close, rather like that of fresh mango, and the taste very slightly peachy with a smoky overtone. Nothing like so sickly as mango. The flesh is a pleasant orange colour. Slice the fruit in half, remove the pippy centre and scoop it from its rind with a spoon.

Cheese Paw Paw

Paw paws
Cottage cheese
Cream cheese
Salt
Lemon juice
Lettuce

Paw Paws, like avocado (see page 85) can also be served with salad dressings and various savoury or mayonnaise mixtures.

Cut the papaya crossways and remove the centre leaving a star shape. Fill this with cream cheese and cottage cheese blended and seasoned to taste with salt and lemon juice. Serve with crisp lettuce.

Paw Paw and Passion Fruit Salad

1 paw paw, seeded, peeled and diced
2 passion fruit
1 orange, peeled and sliced
3 tbspn pineapple pieces
¼ pint pineapple juice or syrup from tin
1 tbspn rum
1 lime

Mix together the diced paw paw flesh from the passion fruit, sliced orange, sliced lime and pineapple pieces. Put enough syrup from the pineapple over the fruit barely to cover it. Or use pineapple juice with extra white sugar. Add the rum and chill thoroughly before serving.

PERSIMMON

Persimmon skin is highly indigestible, but the flesh of this fruit should be eaten fresh or puréed, and is best added to ice cream or custard as it is very astringent.

Persimmon Ice Cream

4 ripe persimmon
2 tbspn sugar
5 tbspn lemon juice
¾ pint double cream

Put the flesh only of the fruit through the electric blender then beat it with the sugar and lemon juice. Whip the cream until it is thick but not buttery and mix it with the sugared purée. Put it in trays in the freezing compartment of the fridge and freeze until set. Do not stir at all while freezing.

Persimmon with Kirsch

Ripe persimmons
Kirsch
Caster sugar

Cut a hole in the top of each fruit and scoop out a little flesh, put some Kirsch and a little sugar in this cavity. Pack the fruit upright in a container so that they cannot spill their dressing, and chill them in the fridge. Make a bed of ice shavings in a bowl and serve the fruit in this, cavity upright.

POMEGRANATES

These round, rosy fruit are about the size of a big orange. They contain yellow flesh full of seeds covered by red jelly, separated by membrane. They are tedious things to eat, needing to be dissected pip by pip and membrane by membrane. One cannot take a good bite at a pomegranate. Nevertheless those who like its light, bitter-sweet taste find it worth the trouble. The seeds are used for flavouring, and the popular continental drink Grenadine is made from pomegranates, as is Mexican Aquardiente.

Each pomegranate renders up quite of lot of juice which is very good spooned over ice cream or with cold milk puddings. See also the recipe for Kumquat Salad (page 89).

SECTION SIX

Bread, Crispbreads, Cereals and Flours

BREAD Many different types of bread can be bought packeted, and specialist delicatessen sell fresh bread of the type eaten in the country they represent. These fresh breads go very well with the food of the country, and because on the whole they are far tastier and more nourishing than our own emasculated bread, make a meal in themselves, when eaten with cheese, salad, olives, sausage, salami, wurst, salt fish, etc., washed down with wine or beer. These breads are often flavoured with seeds—caraway, poppy, sesame—all of which have their own distinctive flavour. All bread is best eaten absolutely fresh, but the darker the bread, the longer it remains palatable. German Pumpernickel, made from whole unbolted rye, and other so-called 'black' breads—Volkornbrot, Linsamerbrot (made from Linseed) keep almost indefinitely as long as they remain wrapped with air excluded. Black bread makes an excellent base for highly flavoured hors d'oeuvres, and is excellent with strong cheese.

Scandinavian crispbreads also retain their flavour and crispness so long as they are kept in airtight containers, and all are good with cheeses, cold meats and hors d'oeuvres. They are too well known to require description.

Scottish readers will forgive me for also including Scottish Oatcakes as an unusual food, but the fact remains that in most of England they are only obtainable from delicatessen. Best eaten with fresh butter, heather honey or marmalade, they also go well with Stilton cheese and Ayrshire cream cheese.

Poppadums are thin lentil biscuits which are eaten as an accompaniment to curry. To cook poppadums drop them into very hot oil; they curl up and expand at the same time and cook instantly. Do one at a time and turn it almost as soon as it hits the hot oil. Remove after about ten seconds and drain off the oil. If the poppadums are very greasy they can be dried off in a slow oven.

Fresh bread, bought or home-made, can be deep frozen and kept for use when required.

FLOUR The white flour we know so well is made from wheat, which has had the outer coat and germ removed during milling. This wheat flour has certain elastic qualities which make it excellent for cakes and bread, qualities which may be lacking in flour made from other grains or pulses. For this reason bread, cakes, pastry, etc., made from these other flours will have quite different textures and may be very heavy. It pays to use at least one part of ordinary wheat flour to each 2 parts of other flours to produce reasonably light dough. There are many varieties of flour producing different flavoured foods. Each country has its favourite. Some of the most popular, usually obtainable at delicatessen, are included here with representative recipes. The basic methods of breadmaking remain the same whatever flour is used.

ATTA FLOUR

Chapatties

8 oz wholemeal or atta flour   Pinch of salt
¼ pint water

Mix the flour and salt and add the water to make a stiff dough. Knead the dough well until it is firm and elastic, then wrap it in greaseproof paper and stand it in a warm place for 30 minutes. Transfer the dough to a floured board and make it into a long roll. Cut this into slices about ½ inch thick. Roll these out into paper-thin rounds. Using a heavy frying pan, a griddle, or even the cooker hot plate (all *ungreased*) cook the chapatties for not more than 1 minute on each side. Then wrap them loosely in a tea towel until cool, and serve immediately. A good accompaniment to curry or chilli dishes.

Atta flour can be bought at Indian food shops and delicatessen.

BUCKWHEAT FLOUR

A variety of Saracen Corn from which a traditional American sweet bread and Russian pancakes are made; a cross between a pancake and a scone.

Blini

Russian pancakes to be eaten with salt fish or caviare.

½ lb buckwheat flour
¼ lb plain white flour
1 oz sugar
1 oz yeast
½ pint warm water

1 oz melted butter
2 eggs
½ tspn salt
½ pint milk
Butter for frying

Mix the yeast to a smooth paste with a little warm water, then add the rest of the warm water and, stirring all the time, the buckwheat flour. Cover this and leave it in a warm place to rise for about half an hour, when it should be double its original size. Beat in the white flour and then the melted butter, egg yolks, sugar and salt. Then stir in the warm milk until the mixture is a smooth batter. Leave this to rise and double. Beat the egg whites until they are really stiff and fold them into the batter. Again leave it to rise and double. Put the batter mixture in separate tablespoonsful on a hot buttered griddle or heavy frying pan.

This makes light thin pancakes, full of holes. Serve them hot covered with melted butter, and, if you wish to be really Russian, sour cream. Blinis are the perfect accompaniment to caviare.

Buckwheat Cakes

½ lb buckwheat flour
⅓ oz yeast
2 tbspn lukewarm water
½ pint milk

½ tspn salt
1 dssrtspn black treacle (molasses)
1 level tspn baking soda

Dissolve the yeast in lukewarm water and leave it to 'start'. Scald the milk and allow it to cool. Mix together the yeast, buckwheat flour, milk and salt and beat the mixture hard for three minutes. Cover it with a tea towel and leave it to stand in a warm room overnight. Next day add the molasses and baking soda, and a little more warm water. The mixture should be runny enough to pour on to a hot griddle in thick pancakes, but not so runny that it spreads out thinly. Grease the griddle first with butter, and brown the cakes on both sides before serving at once with butter and warmed maple syrup. The surface on which you cook, griddle, heavy pan or hot plate, should be just hot enough to make water sprinkled on it sizzle into little balls and disappear.

Buckwheat Cream Cakes

1 lb buckwheat flour	Pinch ground cinnamon
1 tspn salt	¾ pint single cream
1 tbspn caster sugar	1 tspn baking powder

Mix all the ingredients together to a batter, and cook and serve as in previous recipe.

CORNMEAL

Good waterground cornmeal retains its germ and has a superior flavour. It makes light, slightly gritty bread with a rich brown crust. It is usually combined with good plain flour at roughly the proportion of 1½ parts of cornmeal to ½ part plain flour. It is very popular indeed in the United States.

Corn Bread

2 oz plain flour	Big pinch of salt
6 oz cornmeal	1 egg
2½ tspns baking powder	2 tbspn melted butter
2 tbspns sugar	⅓ pint milk

Mix all the dry ingredients together. Beat the egg with the milk and melted butter and combine it with the dry ingredients, do this without excessive beating or stirring. Have ready a baking tin about 9 inches square buttered and sizzling hot. Pour the mixture, which should be a thick batter, into this and bake in a medium hot oven, 420 deg. (gas 6/7) for about 25 minutes.

Cornmeal Porridge

1½ pints boiling water
1 tspn salt
10 oz cornmeal
4 oz butter

Salt the boiling water and stir in the cornmeal. Cook it like porridge until it thickens, then add the butter and let it go on cooking very slowly for another 30 minutes. It will turn into a more or less homogenous lump which does not stick to the pan, and is then ready to eat.

This makes a fairly solid lump of cooked dough which can be eaten by itself, with butter, gravy or grated cheese. It can also be used as accompaniment to beef dishes rather as we use Yorkshire pudding, or plain suet pudding. Always serve it with plenty of rich gravy.

Corn Muffins

Make the same dough as for Corn Bread, and cook it in small buttered and heated patty tins to form many muffins instead of one loaf.

Mexican Tamale Pie (with cornmeal)

1 lb minced beef
1 diced green pepper
1 diced onion
½ tspn oregano
¼ tspn ground cumin
1 tspn salt
2 tspn chilli powder
1 clove garlic
¼ tspn black pepper
1 large tin tomatoes or 1 lb tomatoes
8 oz cornmeal
½ pint water
1½ pint beef stock
Olive oil

Put the meat in a casserole with the onion, pepper and spices and pre-cook it in the oven at 325 deg. (gas 3) for an hour to soften it. Pour off excess fat. Transfer to a frying pan and cook it making sure it does not burn, until the meat is browned. Add the tomatoes and simmer for 20 minutes. Mix the cornmeal with cold water, and then add to it the boiling stock, stirring all the while to prevent lumps. When it thickens, put a layer on the bottom of a fireproof dish, cover this with the meat mixture, and then spread on the rest of the cornmeal mush. Garnish the top of the dish with slices of tomato and cook it in the oven at 375 deg. (gas 5) for about 30 minutes.

Skillet Corn Bread and Bacon Bits

Make a dough exactly as for Corn Bread, and add to it 2 to 4 oz of cooked crisp bacon pieces, chopped small. Put the batter into a heavy covered dish, well buttered and very hot, and cook it as above.

Spoon Bread

2½ oz butter	½ pint cold milk
4 oz cornmeal	2 eggs
1 oz plain flour	½ tspn baking powder
1 tspn salt	or
¾ pint boiling water	4 eggs and no baking powder

Combine the dry ingredients and stir in the boiling water until smooth. Leave it to stand for five minutes and then add milk, and the eggs one at a time, beating the mixture hard after adding each egg. Last of all add the melted butter.

Pour the mixture into a deep fireproof dish in which has been melted a tablespoonful of butter, and cook it for 20 to 30 minutes at 420 deg. gas 6/7.

Serve straight out of the dish with a lot of extra melted butter, or with meat instead of Yorkshire pudding.

HOMINY

Corn with the hull and germ removed. The same grains when broken are called hominy grits.

Hominy Bread

2 oz hominy grits	2 eggs
2 tbspn cream	Pinch salt and white pepper
2 oz cornmeal	2 tspn baking powder
½ oz butter	1 pint boiling water

Stir the grits into boiling salted water and cook just like porridge for 30 minutes. Put the mixture into a bowl and add the butter and beaten egg yolks. Sift in the cornmeal, salt, pepper and baking powder and blend well. Fold in the beaten egg whites, and pour the lot into a buttered fireproof baking dish. Bake for 45 minutes to 1 hour in an oven at 350 deg. (gas 4). Serve it hot with butter, by itself, or with meat and gravy.

MATZO MEAL or CRACKER MEAL

This is made by crushing Matzos, the Jewish unleavened bread. It is used a lot in Jewish cooking.

Matzo Dumplings

¼ pint hot chicken stock
3 egg yolks
3 egg whites
4 tbspn chicken fat or cooking oil
6 oz matzo meal
Pinch salt, ginger, and nutmeg
Tbspn chopped parsley
Tbspn chopped onion

Beat together the egg yolks, chicken fat or oil, then beat in the chicken stock. Stir in the rest of the dry ingredients, then the two well-beaten egg whites. Put the mixture in the fridge for 2 hours, and ½ hour before cooking, make it into little balls. Drop these into boiling soup and simmer, covered, for about 20 minutes until cooked through.

Matzo Omelette

2 eggs
1½ tbsn matzo meal
Salt to taste

Beat well together and pour over any mixture of green and red peppers, onion, garlic, root fennel, aubergines, courgettes, tomatoes, etc., sautéed until soft in butter. Cook for a few minutes longer until the eggs are set, then serve at once. This makes a kind of 'piperade'.

Passover Pasties

½ pint water
¼ pint oil
12 oz matzo meal
6 oz caster sugar
3 eggs
Pinch salt
Big pinch cinnamon
12 oz sweet preserved fruit, or jam
6 oz chopped nuts

Boil the water and oil together and pour it over the mixed matzo meal and sugar, stirring well. Leave it for ½ hour and then add the eggs, one at a time, beating well. Add the seasonings. Form the dough into flat cakes.

Mix together the preserves, nuts and a little matzo meal and put a big spoonful on each piece of dough. Fold over the dough and nip the edges together with your fingers to seal the cake. Flatten it well without bursting it. Fry in hot fat until golden. Serve hot with wine sauce (see page 150).

Scampi or Prawns in Matzo Meal

Coat the drained and dried prawns thoroughly with matzo meal and fry them in butter till brown. Serve hot or cold with sauce tartare (see Page 147).

If you wish to make a thicker coat, first dip the prawns in beaten egg and then coat with the matzo meal.

POTATO FLOUR

Use it as a thickener for gravies, about half as much again as you would plain flour. To avoid it going lumpy, blend the flour with a little sugar before mixing it, or cream it with butter before adding liquid.

Potato Flour Sponge Cake

| 3 oz potato flour | 8 egg yolks |
| 2 oz caster sugar | 8 egg whites |

Mix the flour and sugar and add the thoroughly beaten egg yolks. Beat the egg whites until they are stiff, and fold them into the mixture. Put this into a greased and floured cake tin and cook in a preheated oven at 350 deg. (gas 4) for 40 to 45 minutes.

RICE FLOUR

Used to make close but delicately textured cakes, with lots of eggs in the recipe (see Potato Flour).

Waxy rice flour is very useful for thickening stews, gravies, curries, etc., especially if they are going to be reheated, as rice flour has stabilising powers which prevents the separation of even frozen gravy on reheating.

RYE FLOUR

Rye flour is used much more for bread making on the Continent than it is here, and it produces moist and compact bread, brown with brown crust. It is usually combined with ordinary wheat flour in bread making, to produce less doughy loaves of a lighter colour. Use 10 oz rye flour as a substitute for 8 oz of all-purpose flour.

FINNISH BREAD

2½ oz dried bakers' yeast
3 tspn dark brown sugar
½ oz melted butter
1 tspn salt
½ pint lukewarm water
½ lb plain white flour
6 oz rye flour

Put 2 oz of warm water in a cup and sprinkle the yeast and a teaspoonful of sugar into it. Stir until the yeast is blended in. Leave this for 6 minutes by which time it will be bubbling and should have doubled in volume. Add the rest of the water to the yeast in a large bowl, and using a wooden spoon mix the rest of the sugar, the butter, salt and lastly the white flour and 4 oz of rye flour.

Keep working with the spoon until the dough forms a ball. Then cover the bowl with a tea cloth and let it stand for about 10 minutes, by which time it should have begun to swell a little. Sprinkle a board with a little rye flour if the dough begins to stick to the board. Then make it into a ball again and sprinkle it with flour and put it into a bowl covered with a tea towel and leave it to stand in a warm, draught-free place until it has doubled in bulk, 45 minutes to 1 hour.

Prepare a big flat tin or pastry sheet by buttering and flouring it well.

Remove the dough from the bowl on to the floured board and punch it flat with your fist, and knead it for a few moments. Bake it for 1 hour in an oven at 375 deg. (gas 5). Serve warm with loads of butter.

The Swedes make rye bread the same way, but add more flavourings. Use black treacle instead of brown sugar, and add with the flour 2 tablespoons grated orange peel, 1 tablespoon fennel seed and 1 tablespoon anise seed.

SOY FLOUR

Used to thicken soups and gravies, and in breads, usually in combinations with other flour. Soy flour is high in protein and fat. It causes heavy browning of crusts, so reduce baking temperatures by about 25% when using it.

SECTION SEVEN

Rice and Rice Dishes

There are many varieties of rice available, although generally speaking they fall into three categories—brown unpolished rice (which takes considerably longer to cook than white rice), long grain polished white rice, and short grain polished white rice. Indo-Chinese rice cooks well without breaking up, so is excellent with Chinese dishes. Patna rice is most commonly used to accompany curries, and instead of potatoes with chicken, meat, etc. It is long grained and separates well. Use Italian, Roman or Piedmont rice for risottos. Roman rice is greyish and rather dull, Piedmont is very white, short grained and grey in the centre. Use Carolina rice for puddings and desserts. Java rice goes well with Indonesian dishes. Wild rice (not rice at all really but the seeds of an American water grass) is very good with game.

Rice increases to about four times its original volume when cooked. A large cupful is plenty for three people.

Boiled rice should be stirred as little as possible while it is cooking as this breaks the grains. Most types take about 12 minutes to cook—start testing the rice by nibbling a grain or two after that much time has passed. If rice overcooks it goes mushy and spoils.

To boil rice, add it gradually to plenty of boiling salted water, so that the water does not go off the boil. When it is done, remove it from the heat and drain it in a colander. There are many schools of thought about what should be done next. Some cooks wash the rice under cold running water, then wrap it in a napkin or heap it in the dish in which it is to be served, and put it into a warm oven to reheat for a minute or two. They claim that the grains separate perfectly if the glutinous juice is washed off thus. Rinsing the rice under a hot tap clears away the starch, but the grains do not separate so well.

Rice for risottos is cooked in butter in a frying pan, the dry grains being put in directly, sautéed until brown, when stock, wine, etc., are added and the other ingredients and the rice is cooked to a finish. None of the starch is washed out so the finished dish will be more glutinous and filling than plain boiled rice.

Chinese Fried Rice

This goes with so many things.

¼ pint cooking oil   Boiled rice, drained and dried

Heat the oil in a heavy pan, and add the cooked rice, stir it while it fries, adding more oil if necessary, until each grain is coated and golden. Add to this as much or as little of the following ingredients, according to how savoury you want the rice to be:

Chopped spring onions   Chopped roast pork
Chopped ham   Chopped shrimps

Then, make a well in the middle of the rice and break at least one egg into the middle, and with the pan over a medium heat, stir the eggs with a fork until they begin to scramble, keeping them in the well until they begin to set, then stir them out into the rice. Sprinkle a little soy sauce on top and serve immediately.

Cumin Rice

Before serving, dust the heap of plain boiled rice with ground cumin.

Paella

The Spanish version of risotto, made with a variety of ingredients, some of which in this country are hard to get outside a delicatessen.

1 lb long grain rice
12 mussels
½ small chicken
1 tin calamares (octopus)
½ lb frozen peas
1 tin prawns, or packet of frozen prawns
1 tin lobster meat or ½ a fresh lobster
¼ lb chorizo sausage
4 tbspn chopped parsley

2 tbspn chopped onion
½ lb lean pork in small cubes
¼ pint olive oil
4 cloves garlic, chopped
6 tomatoes, or 1 tin
2 green peppers
1 red pepper
Salt and black pepper
1 pint chicken stock
½ tspn saffron
Dry white wine

If you add up the volume of all these ingredients, you will find that it comes to a very big heap, so you will need a huge frying pan or a proper paella pan to cook them in.

Steam the mussels in wine with a little chopped onion, until they open, but strain them to keep the liquor. Add a little more wine and poach the calamares, cut into pieces, for a few minutes. Strain and keep the liquor. Sauté all the meat pieces in olive oil until they are golden, remove them and sauté the lobster and prawns in the same oil. Remove them and sauté the rest of the onion, the chopped peppers and garlic. Add the tomatoes and simmer together. Keep back some of the prawns and mussels for garnish, but put all the other cook ingredients back into the pan, and add the mussel liquor.

Mix the saffron with the stock and pour it over the contents of the pan. Bring it to the boil and add the rice. Cook it without a lid on for 15 minutes, then add the green peas, stir well, and then garnish it with the rest of the seafood and leave it to cook without disturbing it for another 15 minutes, or until the rice is tender. Serve the paella in the pan in which it has been cooked.

Risotto

Almost anything can go into risotto; green or red peppers, chopped celery, chicken livers, shrimps, mussels, prawns, chicken meat, either singly or in combinations, which means that it is a wonderful way to use up left-overs.

1 large onion	Little saffron
2 oz mushrooms	2 wineglassfuls white wine
2 slices cooked ham	Pinch nutmeg
Parmesan cheese	1 large cupful Italian rice
1 pint chicken stock	¼ lb butter

Chop the onion and sauté it in the butter. Add the rice and let it cook for about 5 minutes, shaking the pan continuously until it is brown. Add the wine and continue cooking over a low heat until it is absorbed. Then add two-thirds of the stock. While the risotto is cooking, put the saffron—3 or 4 stamens ground to a powder should be enough—into the rest of the stock with the nutmeg, and add it after about 10 minutes, with the chopped mushrooms and chopped ham. When the rice is cooked, stir in a dessertspoonful of grated Parmesan cheese, and serve at once, before the rice cools and goes sticky, with another sprinkling of Parmesan on top.

Any other ingredients which need a little cooking should be sautéed with the onion, and the saffron can be left out if you do not like it.

Saffron Rice
To make saffron rice, take a pinch of dried saffron and bruise it, then add it to the water in which the rice is boiled.

Sweet Spiced Pulao

1 lb rice	4 oz sultanas
3 oz butter	½ tspn mace
3 cardamon seeds	½ tspn cinnamon
6 cloves	1½ tbspn sugar
4 oz blanched almonds	Salt to taste

Melt the butter and brown the rice in it. Add all the other ingredients with enough water to cover the rice, and boil it slowly until the rice is done. Add more water during cooking if necessary.

Wild Rice baked in Consommé

½ lb raw wild rice	1 tbspn butter
1 can condensed consommé	1 tbspn sherry
½ lb sliced mushrooms	

Wash the rice well in several changes of cold water, removing all the odd bits and pieces. Put it in a greased casserole. Add the consommé and sherry and stir it well. Leave the dish to stand for 3 hours. Bake it in the oven at 350 deg. (gas 4) for 45 minutes, adding a little water if it gets too dry. Sauté the mushrooms in butter for about 5 minutes and put them on top of the rice. Turn the oven down a little and cook until the rice has absorbed the liquid.

SECTION EIGHT

Pasta and Popcorn

PASTA Macaroni, spaghetti, vermicelli, crescioni, ditalini, fedilini, ravioli, reginette, stricetti, tagliarini, tagliatelli, tortellini; there are at least fifty-two varieties, and in each district of Italy identical pastas have different names. However, they do come in five main categories, and within those categories their uses are much the same:

> *Long Pasta*—long strips of pasta in various sizes, in tubes and strips, usually served with Neopolitan (tomato) sauce, Bolognese (meat) sauce, or Pesto, or with plenty of butter and cheese and black pepper stirred in (see pages 144-146).
> *Short Pasta*—use these with the same sauces and also in soups. These big pastas carry a lot of sauce and absorb a lot of liquid, so are used in substantial soups and with plenty of thick sauces.
> *Small Pasta*—little stars and thin pieces of all kinds which are solely used for adding to clear soups and broths to make more of a meal of them.
> *Large Pasta*—large, flat, tube-shaped pieces, meant to be used after boiling, to make up various dishes which will be further cooked in the oven.
> *Filled pasta*—there are varieties, such as ravioli or tortellini, which are usually served as a separate dish, but sometimes put into soups.

Egg Pasta (pasta all'uovo) is made by adding dry or fresh eggs to the basic mixture of durum wheat flour, semolina and water. The slightly yellow colour of ordinary pasta is due to the addition of turmeric or to various chemical colourings. *Green Pasta* (pasta verde) is coloured with spinach, but sometimes the green pasta has artificial colouring. This is stated on the packet, and should be left well alone.

Pasta made in Naples is supposed to be the finest in the world. Pasta is usually bought dried in packets, and keeps for ages.

Cooking: Allow 3-4 oz of pasta per serving. Drop it dry into boiling salted water. Use 1 quart of water and 1 tablespoonful of salt per 1 lb of pasta. Cook it, boiling steadily, from 7 to 15 minutes, depending on the type of pasta, until it is *'al dente'*, that is slightly chewy, but tender. Never cook it to a soft mush. Take the saucepan from the stove and pour in a cupful of cold water to stop it cooking, and drain the pasta immediately. Then add a knob of butter or a little olive oil, and stir it or shake it gently to make sure it is well coated, before using it as your particular recipe demands—with a sauce, or other additions.

Having boiled lasagne or cannelloni or any pasta which you intend to separate and fill or otherwise handle, drain it and put it in a colander and run cold water over it. Make sure that the water gets well between the pieces. They will not then stick together during the time it takes to make up the dish.

Cannelloni

½ lb cannelloni
¼ lb mushrooms
¼ lb minced ham
¼ lb minced veal, beef or mutton
1 small chopped onion
Olive oil
¼ lb grated cheese
1 pint Béchamel sauce (see page 140)
Parmesan cheese
Butter

Boil the cannelloni tubes and fill them with a mixture of mushrooms, ham, veal and onion, which have been previously fried in a little olive oil, until they are well blended and soft. Lay the stuffed cannelloni in neat rows in a buttered fireproof dish, or in pairs in small individual dishes. Make a good cheese sauce, preferably using Parmesan cheese, but failing that any good cooking cheese. Add it to the Béchamel sauce, and when mixed pour it over the cannelloni. Sprinkle a little Parmesan cheese on the top and cook in a moderate oven until the cheese is bubbling. Alternatively finish the individual dishes off under a fast grill.

Cannelloni can also be made out of Lasagne, by rolling the pieces of flat pasta round the filling.

Lasagne

These are large strips of pasta, either plain or verdi (green). They are usually served with Italian sausage or meat balls, lots of cheese, hard-boiled egg and rich Neapolitan sauce (see page 144), put in layers in a fireproof dish, topped off with cheese and baked until the cheese is bubbling.

1 lb lasagne	Tomato sauce (see page 144)
½ lb Mozarella and ½ lb Ricotta, or 1 lb mild Cheddar cheese	Salt and pepper
	Olive oil
	¼ lb Italian sausage or meat balls
2 oz grated Parmesan	
3 hard-boiled eggs	

Grease a small fireproof dish with butter and line it with cooked lasagne. Then add a layer of chopped sausage, a layer of mozarella or Cheddar, a layer of hard-boiled egg, then some Ricotta or more Cheddar and a little Parmesan. Pour a good layer of tomato sauce over the lot and sprinkle a little more Parmesan on the top.

You can make this dish in separate fireproof dishes in which it is individually served, or in one big dish, with the layers repeated until all the ingredients are used up, and from which it can be spooned on to plates. It is really best served individually and undisturbed, as the act of spooning it on to plates mixes up all the layers and rather spoils the effect.

Of course Italian cheese makes the dish that much better, but at a pinch the substitution of English cheese will still produce a very pleasant meal, but do top off with Parmesan.

Small meat balls can be substituted for the Italian sausage, and green or yellow lasagne can be used. The hard-boiled egg is not strictly necessary.

Spaghetti served with Bolognese Sauce

Boil the spaghetti, drain it, add oil, heap it on heated plates, pour Bolognese sauce (see below) over the top, and finish with a sprinkling of Parmesan cheese.

If you wish to cook spaghetti in long pieces rather than breaking it, take a handful and put the loose ends in fast-boiling water in the saucepan. As the pasta heats, it softens quite quickly, and can be gently pushed and curled in round the pan, and the last few ends poked down with a fork.

Bolognese Sauce

½ lb minced beef or tin of minced beef
¼ lb chopped green bacon or salt pork or ham
2 oz chicken livers
1 chopped onion
1 chopped carrot
1 small tin tomato purée
½ pint stock
¼ pint white wine
Pinch nutmeg
1 bay leaf
2 oz butter or olive oil
Salt and black pepper
Cream

If fresh mince is used, cook this in a covered casserole slowly for about an hour. Drain off the surplus fat. Fry the bacon, onion, carrot, and chicken livers in the butter. Add the minced beef when these have cooked a little, add the tomato purée, stock, wine, nutmeg, bay leaf and salt and pepper. Cover the pan and simmer slowly for about 30 minutes, stirring occasionally. Add 2 tablespoonfuls of fresh cream just before serving.

As many of the ingredients as possible should be included, but these can be altered slightly if necessary.

Spatzen or Spatzle

2 eggs
6 oz S.R. flour
½ pint water
Big pinch salt
Pinch nutmeg

Beat all the ingredients well together, and drop the mixture into simmering stock, salted water or soup. This can be done by pouring the batter through a colander with big holes, through a grater with big holes, or, rather more tediously, drop by drop with a saltspoon. Spatzle must be light, and if the mixture is too thick and heavy it will not go through the colander. Thin the mixture with water, and test by making just a few.

If Spatzle are to be served as an accompaniment, then drain them when they are cooked and stir a knob of butter and a dash of pepper and salt on to them before serving. Put directly into soup, they can be served floating in it.

Tagliatelli or Fettuccine

Cook as usual, then stir in a lot of butter and cheese, and leave it for a little while to soak in. Serve more butter and cheese at the table.

POPCORN

A variety of corn which, when heated expands and explodes to make white fluffy granules. It can be bought in tins ready to 'pop'. Use a heavy-based saucepan with a well-fitting lid. Put a knob of butter in it and stand it over heat. After a minute, put about a quarter of a cupful of corn in the pan and put on the lid. Shake the pan over the heat, and after a moment or two the corn will start to pop. Keep shaking the pan over the heat until the popping ceases. Remove from the heat, leave to stand for a few moments, then take off the lid. (If you take off the lid while the pan is still over the heat, you may get popcorn all over the kitchen.) Pick out any imperfect or unpopped grains of corn.

Pour the popcorn out into a bowl and shake some salt over it, and eat it straight away. More melted butter can be added if liked.

If the corn will not pop, it has got too dry in the can. Put it in a closed jar with two tablespoonfuls of water, shake it well and let it stand for a few days, then try again, but if it stands for too long it will go mouldy.

Candied Popcorn

½ cupful of corn
1 tbspn butter
1 cup moist brown sugar
4 tbspn water
(Cooking thermometer)

Mix the ingredients (except the corn) together in a saucepan and bring to the boil, stirring frequently. Cover it and cook for 3 minutes. Uncover the pan and cook without stirring until it reaches 238 deg. F. (Softball). Take it off the heat and stir the popped corn in gently with a wooden spoon until it is all well coated. Allow it to cool before eating it.

SECTION NINE

Pulses

CHICK PEAS

A kind of lentil used as a basic ingredient of soups and stews all round the Mediterranean. Dried chick peas must be soaked overnight in water containing a handful of salt, then cooked for several hours in plenty of water to soften them. If you have a pressure cooker you will be able to reduce the cooking time considerably.

Chick Peas and Chorizos

1 lb chick peas	1 tspn olive oil
Bouquet garni	Spanish chorizo sausage
Small hock or piece of bacon	5 tbspn tomato purée
Salt and pepper	1 clove garlic

Soak and cook the chick peas with the bouquet garni and the bacon, salt and pepper and the oil, until they are soft. Drain the peas and remove the hock and the bouquet garni. Cut the lean meat off the hock into pieces and return it to the peas with the chopped chorizo, tomato purée and crushed garlic. Moisten with some of the liquid in which the peas were cooked, put the lot in the oven in a covered casserole and let it cook together for another hour. This is really a Spanish version of bacon and beans.

Chick Peas and Egg

4 oz tinned chick peas	4 eggs
Butter	Salt and pepper
1 onion	Little cream
8 black olives	Chopped parsley

Dice the onion and stone the olives and sauté them in butter until the onion 'melts' without browning. Add the drained chick peas and cook for a few minutes until the peas are heated. Add the beaten eggs, and stir until they begin to scramble, add the cream and salt and pepper to taste. Finish the scrambling, but do not let the mixture get too dry, it should still be pleasantly moist. Garnish each serving with chopped parsley.

Chick Peas in Spanish Tomato Sauce

Soak and cook the peas until they are tender, and serve them with tomato sauce (see page 148), or any well-flavoured sauce that you like.

Hummus Bi Tahina, Humous V'Tahina

Served as a first course in many Greek and Middle Eastern restaurants in London, this appetiser is very easy to make. It is possible to buy hummus mix to which it is only necessary to add oil, water and tahina, in Greek grocers' shops in London, where you can also buy the tahina ready made (or see page 149).

½ lb chick peas, cooked until very soft
¼ pint tahina
¼ pint olive oil
¼ pint water
Juice of 1 lemon
2 big cloves garlic
2 tbspn mint (ommitted in some recipes)
Salt and pepper

Drain the chick peas and pound them to a smooth paste in a liquidiser with the garlic, then add all the ingredients except the mint and salt and pepper and beat thoroughly together. Then stir in the mint, season to taste, and serve with hot bread. Or omit the mint, sprinkle the hummus with chopped parsley, and garnish it with sliced radish, cucumber, olives, pickled chillis, or any other salad ingredient you like

Salted Chick Peas

Soak and cook the chick peas until they are tender, but not mushy or broken up. Drain them and sprinkle them thoroughly with salt and freshly ground black pepper. Serve them to be eaten just like salted peanuts.

LENTILS

There are lentils in all shades from white to black, via yellow, red, brown and green. They are all cooked in more or less the same way. First they should be washed and any odd bits and pieces removed. Then leave them to soak in cold water overnight. Drain them, and put them in plenty of cold water and heat to simmering point. Remove scum from the surface and continue cooking until the water is clear, then add herbs and spices and any other additions, and continue cooking until done. Lentils can be cooked until they are a completely soft purée, or until they are soft but still whole.

Brown Continental lentils look and taste very different from the yellow split peas we buy as lentils in our grocers' shops. Brown lentils do not break up into a porridge, but even when soft remain fairly separate. They make an excellent accompaniment to any kind of hot smoked sausage, bacon or ham.

Brown Lentil Soup

½ lb lentils
2 rashers lean bacon
1 small onion
1 clove garlic

Salt and pepper
Olive oil
Butter

Soak and boil the lentils until they are tender, but only salt the water very lightly. Chop the onion and garlic and sauté them in a little butter until soft, add the chopped bacon, and cook for a few minutes, but do not crisp. Add these to the lentils and continue cooking until the lentils are very soft and the mixture is the consistency of soup. Spoon the soup into bowls and swirl in a tablespoonful of olive oil into each plateful. Grind a liberal sprinkling of fresh black pepper on top and serve with crusty bread.

Dahl

There are many varieties of dahl lentil, but the three commonest are: TOOR DAHL, medium size, orange lentil, available both dry and oily. Buy the oily type if you can get it. MOONG DAHL is a small yellow type, and CHAMMA DAHL is a medium-sized fawn coloured lentil. These must be cooked until soft and then aromatised with curry spices.

½ lb lentils
¾ pint water
4 oz coconut milk
1 sliced green chilli
¼ tspn ground cumin

¼ tspn ground black pepper
½ tspn turmeric
1 large chopped onion
1 crushed clove garlic
1 chopped green pepper

Put all the ingredients together except the coconut milk (see page 133) and salt, until the lentils are completely soft, and everything is well blended. If you like dahl really smooth, put the cooked mixture through an electric blender. Add the coconut milk, season to taste with salt and reheat and serve, either as a dish by itself, or as an accompaniment to curry.

Lentils and Bacon

Lentils	Pepper
Celery	Salt
Bacon	

Allow 3 oz of brown lentils per serving. Soak them overnight and then cook them in salted boiling water with several stalks of celery—use odd pieces not good enough for eating with cheese—for about an hour and a half until soft but not mushy. Chop two rashers of fat unsmoked bacon and cook them in a frying pan until they have released their fat, then add the lentils and a little of the liquid they were cooked in, season with pepper and simmer for a few minutes until most of the liquid has been absorbed.

Lentils and Salt Pork

½ lb brown lentils	Parsley
½ lb salt pork	Crushed garlic
1 oz butter	Lemon juice
1 sliced onion	Salt
Bay leaf	Parsley

Soak the lentils for an hour and drain them. Put the onion into a heavy pan and cook it in the butter until soft. Add the piece of pork, lentils, 2½ pints water, garlic and bay leaf. Put the pan on a very low heat and let it simmer without the lid on until the water has been nearly absorbed. There should still be enough left to make a gravy around the meat when it is served. Remove the pork and cut it into serving pieces. Add lemon juice, salt and black pepper to the lentils to taste. Put the pork pieces on a hot dish, pour the lentils over and sprinkled chopped parsley on top as garnish. Serve with crusty bread and red wine.

A piece of bacon can be used instead of the salt pork.

This is a standard French country recipe and makes a tasty and filling meal.

RED HARICOT BEANS (tinned or dried)

The tinned variety may be used straight out of the tin, but dried beans must be soaked before use. A two hour soaking in cold water is enough. Longer soaking may allow a slight fermentation to start which alters the taste. The purpose of soaking is to replace the moisture lost in drying processes, not to soften the beans; this must be done by cooking them. Red beans are an essential ingredient of Chilli con carne, and, like all beans, go well with pork or bacon.

To cook dried beans: Put the pre-soaked beans into a big saucepan with plenty of cold water, and bring it to the boil, skim it, cover the saucepan and simmer very slowly until the beans are soft but not mushy. Check from time to time that the beans have not boiled dry. To improve the flavour add salt and pepper, an onion stuck with cloves, and a bouquet garni. Salt bacon, pieces of pork skin and fat or a knuckle of pork, added to the simmering beans will help to enrich and flavour them.

Chilli Con Carne

1 tin or ½ lb red beans
1 tin stewing beef or ½ lb stewing beef
1 tin or 1 lb tomatoes
1 large onion
Chilli powder
1 clove garlic
Cooking oil
1 tspn oregano
Big pinch cumin
Plain flour

To make a quick chilli con carne, chop and sauté the onion and garlic in a big heavy frying pan, add a tin of stewing steak, and cook it for 5 minutes, then add a tin of tomatoes and a tin of beans with their liquor. Add the seasonings, and chilli powder to taste. It depends on the strength of the chilli powder and the degree of heat you can take, just how much. A heaped teaspoonful of good chilli powder is enough for most British palates, but up to a tablespoonful can be added if you can take it.

To make the dish from fresh ingredients, first sauté the

onion, then chop the meat into small pieces and roll it in seasoned plain flour, and brown it in the pan with the onions, adding more oil if necessary. Add the crushed garlic and the other seasonings including the chilli powder and the pre-cooked beans, with enough of the cooking liquor just to cover the contents of the pan. Skin the tomatoes and add them. Let the mixture cook very slowly for at least half an hour, until all the ingredients are well blended and the gravy is thick, and the meat tender.

To make more of either dish, add up to 1 lb of fresh, frozen or tinned broad beans.

Fried Red Beans and Bacon

½ pint red wine
½ lb precooked or tinned red beans

8 lean rashers bacon

Cut the bacon into pieces and fry it. Add the beans and the red wine, and cook until most of the moisture has been used up and the gravy is fairly thick. Serve as a supper dish.

SECTION TEN

Cheese and Other Milk Products

BUTTERMILK

Milk from which the butterfat has been removed by churning, but which retains all the mineral salts and some of the lactose present in milk. A proportion of the lactose will have been used up as some lactic acid fermentation has taken place. It is much drunk in America and on the continent for its health-giving qualities, especially by slimmers who don't want butterfat. It has only recently been marketed on any scale in this country and can be bought natural or fruit flavoured just like yoghurt. The fruit-flavoured buttermilk is best drunk just as it is; and natural buttermilk may be used in any of the following recipes:

Buttermilk Biscuits

10 oz SR flour
1 tspn salt
¼ tspn soda

4 tbspn butter
Buttermilk

Mix the dry ingredients together and rub in the butter. Add enough buttermilk to make dough. Knead for a moment or two only on a floured board. Press and pat it down to ¼ inch thick and cut it into rounds with a pastry cutter. Put the biscuits on a greased tin and bake for 10-12 minutes until they have risen and browned a little.

Buttermilk Cornbread

6 oz SR flour
½ tspn baking soda
1 tbspn sugar
1 tspn salt
4 oz cornmeal (see page 101)

½ pint buttermilk
2 eggs
4 tbspns melted butter or bacon fat
1 tbspn salt pork crackling

Mix all the dry ingredients and add buttermilk and melted fat.

When this is blended together add the pork cracklings. The bread is fine without this last ingredient but if available they do add a little something. Pour the mixture into a flat tin and cook for about half an hour in a medium oven (350 deg., gas 4).

Buttermilk Drink

An excellent nourishing drink for invalids or for those with digestive trouble can be made by blending a tablespoonful of any plain cereal flour with a quart of buttermilk. Put the mixture in a non-stick pan and allow it to simmer down to a quarter of its original volume. Sweeten it to taste.

Cold Buttermilk Soup

3 egg yolks
¼ lb caster sugar or vanilla sugar

2 lemons
1½ pint plain buttermilk
Whipped cream (optional)

Beat the egg yolks and add the sugar gradually until the mixture thickens. Add the rind of the lemon without white pith, very thinly grated, and a teaspoonful of lemon juice. Beat until the mixture is really smooth. Chill the soup and serve it with a spoonful of cream on top (although this rather negates the idea of cream-free buttermilk) and accompanied by oatcakes (see page 98).

CHEESE

Every country produces its own cheeses and there are so many of these imported into this country that it is impossible to list them all here. I think it best just to list some that are used not only to eat 'straight' with bread, etc., but also in cooked dishes. *Parmesan* is a splendid hard cooking cheese, with a strong sharp taste which goes well with pasta and tomatoes. It is usually used grated very fine and is excellent for topping off any dish to be browned in the oven, soups, spaghetti bolognese, etc. *Gruyère*, *Emmenthaler*, and *Jarlsberg* are the best cheeses for making fondue. They go delightfully sticky and stringy when cooked. *Mozzarella* is a good soft Italian cooking cheese, and *Bel Paese* will substitute for it. *Roquefort* is a beautiful blue cheese from France, best eaten straight, but excellent for salad dressing (see page 146). *Ayrshire Cream Cheese* is really very slightly cheesy cream and is marvellous added to soup in large dollops, and is also very good with sweet fruit such as strawberries. For recipes that demand *Ricotta*, *Philadelphia* is a good substitute. *English Cheddar* is a good substitute for Parmesan and other hard cheese in oven-baked dishes. It can also be used for French onion soup, but will not go sticky and stringy like Gruyère. *Danish Blue* is useful for hors d'oeuvre and small snacks which require a very strong salty cheese. *Cottage Cheese* is low in calories and very useful for dressings, beaten up with milk or buttermilk, salt, wine vinegar, and onion and herbs if liked.

To keep cheese in good condition, store it carefully. Hard cheese will keep in good condition if you butter the cut edges before wrapping it in foil or putting it in a refrigerator. Always wrap cheese in foil before refrigerating it, or its smell may contaminate other foods in the fridge. Of course, if you like your cheese ripe, do not store it in the fridge. The French eat their *Camembert* while it is still crumbly and white, and only just softening, but we prefer it getting yellow and runny and rather smelly. Camembert when bought should just yield to pressure in the centre of the cheese, as should *Brie* and *Coulommier* and other similar cheeses. To bring them to the degree of runniness we prefer, they may be kept on a larder shelf for a day or two, not in a fridge. If the cheese has been bought in its own box or carton, do not disturb it till you wish to eat it. If it has been bought by the piece from a larger cheese, then wrap it in foil immediately upon getting it home.

Cheese Cake

½ lb chocolate-covered wheatmeal biscuits
4 tbspn butter
12 oz cream cheese
3 tbspn caster sugar
1 tspn vanilla essence
Juice and rind of ½ lemon, or whole lemon if the cheese is bland

2 egg yolks
½ oz powdered gelatine
3 egg whites
½ pint double cream

Combine the crumbled biscuits and warmed softened butter, and press into the bottom of a loose bottomed 9-inch cake tin.

Bake for 15 minutes at 300 deg. (gas 2). Allow to cool completely.

Combine the cream cheese, sugar and vanilla. Grate the lemon rind (without pith) and add it and the juice with the beaten egg yolks. Whisk all well together, and immediately add the gelatine dissolved in 2 tablespoonsful of warm water. Then beat the egg whites very stiffly and fold them into the cheese mixture. Whip the cream and fold it in. Spoon this evenly over the crust and chill for several hours before carefully transferring the cheese cake to a plate.

Garnish the top with piped whipped cream and grated chocolate if you wish to make it even fancier and richer.

This very rich but easily made dessert should be made with good quality cream cheese.

Cream Cheese Pancakes

4 oz Camembert, Brie or Ricotta cheese
½ oz butter
½ pint thick Béchamel sauce (see page 140)
A pile of small thin pancakes

1 onion
1 small tin tomatoes
1 dssrtspn tomato purée
1 tbspn olive oil
Salt and pepper
Grated Parmesan

Discard the rind and mash the cheese well into the Béchamel sauce. This mixture must be firm and not runny. Spread a thick layer on each pancake and then roll them up like little Swiss rolls, and pack them into a fireproof dish.

Chop the onion and cook it in oil until it is soft but not brown. Add the tomatoes and tomato purée and the seasonings. Cook this for a few minutes then put it through an electric blender until it is absolutely smooth. Pour it over the rolled pancakes and sprinkle just a little grated Parmesan on the top. Cook in the top of a hot oven until it is brown and bubbling. Serve immediately.

Fondue

½ lb Gruyère
½ lb Emmenthaler
1 tspn cornflour
1 clove fresh garlic
2 cups dry white wine

Salt and pepper
Nutmeg
Paprika
French bread
3 tbspn kirsch

Use a chafing dish or a casserole which can be put directly over a low flame. Special fondue-making pots can be bought—they look very nice but are not essential.

Rub the inside of the dish with the cut garlic. Pour in the wine and heat it very slowly until the bubbles begin to rise, but do not boil it. Grate the cheese and add it to the wine bit by bit, stirring clockwise ceaselessly and allowing the cheese to melt before adding more. Dissolve the cornflour in the kirsch and add this to the cheese, stirring well. Season the fondue to taste and it is ready to serve. If you have a hotplate which will keep it bubbling all the better, stand it on this. Otherwise use a small table spirit lamp and stand.

Provide everyone with a fork. Cut the bread into chunks big enough to be firmly speared by the fork. Dunk the bread on the fork in the fondue with a stirring movement, and be careful not to burn your mouth. If the fondue thickens too much at this stage, add a little warmed wine.

Mozzarella In Carrozza

Slices of cheese	2 tbspn dry white wine
Thin slices white bread	Frying oil
Eggs	Salt and pepper

This is a wonderful snack meal, and is remarkably filling. Just make sandwiches with the cheese and bread from which the crusts have been removed. Pinch the edges of each sandwich together so that it will stay in one piece during cooking. Beat up a couple of eggs, or more according to the number of snacks you are making, add the wine, and let the sandwiches soak in the liquid until they are saturated, which should take about ¼ hour. Heat the oil in a frying pan until it is smoking, then fry the sandwiches quickly and eat them straight out of the pan as soon as they are golden brown, sprinkled with salt and pepper. If you have got the temperature of the fat right, the bread-soaked egg will be crisp and golden and the cheese just melted inside.

Parmesan Meringues

2 tbspn grated Parmesan cheese	Salt and pepper
2 egg whites	

Whisk the egg whites until they are very stiff then fold in the cheese and seasonings. Drop this mixture a tablespoonful at a time into very hot cooking oil in a deep frying pan. The meringues take only 2 or 3 minutes to turn golden brown, and should be drained and eaten at once. Delicious as a snack on their own or with crisply grilled bacon.

Quiche Lorraine

This is egg and cheese pie which can often be bought ready-made in delicatessen, but is extremely easy to make at home. It is best made with Gruyère cheese, or with a mixture of blue cheese (Roquefort, Danish or Gorgonzola) and cottage cheese.

4 oz flaky pastry (make your own or use ready-made)
4 oz chopped lean bacon
4 oz sliced Gruyère

3 eggs
¼ pint thin cream
Salt and pepper

Line a well-buttered sandwich cake tin or a shallow fireproof dish with the pastry. Put the bacon in a bowl and pour boiling water over it and leave it for a few minutes to poach, then drain and dry. Put the thinly sliced cheese in the pastry case with the bacon pieces in layers. Beat the eggs and cream together, season with salt and pepper, and pour over the cheese and bacon. Bake at 400 deg. (gas 6) for 30 minutes, by which time the egg should be golden and well risen.

To make a different variety, substitute 3 oz Blue cheese and 6 oz Cottage cheese for the Gruyère, mix it together and blend it into the beaten eggs. Substitute 1 onion cut into very thin rings and sautéd until soft in butter, for the bacon. Lay this in the pastry case and pour in the cheese and egg mixture. Cook as above.

There are many different recipes for Quiche. Some recommend making Béchamel sauce (see page 140), blending in grated cheese and beaten eggs and bacon pieces, and filling the pastry case with this. It will not be so light as the previous mixtures as it contains flour, but on the other hand will be more filling.

SOUR CREAM

Make sour cream by adding lemon to fresh farm cream and standing it for a while until it thickens.

Cream which has been pasteurised will not sour without the addition of special culture. Sour cream can be bought in cartons in some delicatessen. Natural yoghurt is a good substitute.

YOGHURT

Milk fermented with a special culture produces yoghurt, which twenty years ago was almost unknown except to health food addicts. This excellent food is now sold by every dairy, every grocers' shop with a fridge; every health food shop and most delicatessen. Factory-made yoghurt, which is what you buy in shops, is made from evaporated milk with or without its cream and is not so sharp or strong as home-made yoghurt. However, for the purposes of this book, it is the shop varieties we are interested in. Yoghurt can be bought flavoured with all kinds of fruit, nuts, chocolate, coffee, etc., but in many ways it is better to buy natural yoghurt and flavour it to taste.

Add fruit syrups, or spoonful of any kind of jam you like. Add maple syrup and honey, blend drinking chocolate powder to a paste with a little milk and mix it in. Add chopped nuts with maple syrup or honey. Add coffee essence, with or without nuts.

Use yoghurt as a substitute for sour cream in any recipe.

Yoghurt and Apple Breakfast

Natural yoghurt
Chopped crisp apple
Muesli

Put the chopped apple into a bowl, add as many spoonful of yoghurt as you fancy, sprinkle the top with Muesli, and eat at once, before the apple changes colour.

Yoghurt and Cucumber Salad

Very finely sliced cucumber	1 tspn caster sugar
Dssrtspn natural yoghurt	Juice of 1 lemon
Dssrtspn thin cream or top of the milk	½ tspn dried dill
	Pinch salt

Put the sliced cucumber in a colander and sprinkle it with salt. Leave it for an hour and then press it with a saucer to extract more water. Dry the cucumber gently in a clean cloth. Mix the other ingredients together, doubling up quantities to make sufficient to cover the amount of cucumber you intend to serve. Pour the dressing all over the cucumber so that it is well coated.

Serve as a 'sambal' or side dish with curry, as an hors d'oeuvre or with salmon or smoked salmon.

Yoghurt, just as it is, makes an excellent sauce for Dolmades (stuffed vine leaves, see page 84). See also Shrimp Artichoke salad (page 54).

SECTION ELEVEN

Nuts and Seeds

Many different kinds of nuts can be bought from delicatessen—fresh, dried, roasted, ground, or in tins. It would be possible to produce a cookery book containing nothing but nut recipes, and I have to limit myself here to one or two useful recipes for each type of nut.

To Blanch Nuts

To remove the inner skin of nuts after they have been shelled, pour water over them in a bowl, and drain them almost immediately. The skins should rub off between the fingers. Peanuts and pistachio nuts can be blanched this way, but are usually roasted in their skins for about 10 minutes. The dry skins are then rubbed off.

To Roast Nuts

Put the nuts in an oven at about 300 deg. (gas 2) and cook until they are crisp. The length of time depends upon the nut, but if they are over-cooked they go tough. Roast nuts are done when they take on a nice golden-brown colour, but are over-done when they are dark brown or scorched. To roast and salt nuts, put a little olive oil in a bowl and shake the nuts around in this until they are coated. Add ½ teaspoonful of salt per ½ lb nuts, shake well and spread the nuts in a flat tin and roast at 250 deg. (gas ½) for 10 to 15 minutes.

ALMONDS

Almonds can be blanched and whole, or blanched and roasted and salted, or ground to make marzipan. They can also be ground into butter in an electric blender without additional oil.

Almond Halva

6 oz semolina	4 oz butter
6 oz ground almonds	3 eggs
14 oz sugar	1 tspn ground cinnamon
Water	Lemon juice or rosewater

Beat the butter and 8 oz of sugar together until white and creamy, then add the well beaten eggs, cinnamon, ground almonds and semolina. Beat the mixture well together and pour it into a buttered baking dish. Cook it in a moderate oven for an hour. Make a syrup with the rest of the sugar, a scant ½ pint of water and a little rosewater or the juice of 1 lemon, by cooking them together until they begin to thicken. Pour this syrup over the halva and serve immediately.

Candied Almonds

¼ lb blanched almonds   2 tbspn clear honey
¼ lb caster sugar

Put the honey and sugar together in a heavy pan over a low heat, and being careful not to burn the mixture, cook it until it changes colour and caramelises. Add the almonds and continue to cook until a drop or two of the mixture forms a hard ball in cold water. Pour it on to a cold marble slab, or into a shallow buttered tin. Break it into pieces when it has set hard.

Fillets of sole with Shredded Almonds

Fillets of Sole   Salt and pepper
Milk   Lemon
Flour   Parsley
Butter

Dip the fish fillets in milk and dust them with flour, and sauté them in plenty of butter until cooked and nicely browned. Make a sauce by melting more butter and shredding into it blanched almonds until you have enough to put a good coating over the fish. Serve with parsley and lemon wedges.

BRAZIL NUTS

Cover the kernels with cold water, and bring to the boil and simmer for 5 minutes. Drain the nuts and slice them lengthwise on a vegetable slicer, which makes little curls. Put the slices on an oven sheet and roast them at 350 deg. (gas 4) for 10 minutes. Salt and serve.

CASHEW NUTS

These must always be eaten roasted, as this destroys a poison which the raw nuts contain.

Cashew Nut Butter

½ lb lightly roasted cashew nuts
2 tbspn sunflower, peanut or other tasteless vegetable oil (see page 145)

Salt

Put the nuts and oil into an electric blender and beat it up until it reaches the texture you like, coarse or smooth, and add salt to taste.

Cashews à la Diable

Fry the nuts in butter until they are golden brown, strain them and sprinkle with cayenne pepper and salt, and serve as a savoury or hors d'oeuvre.

COCONUT MILK

Coconut milk is an ingredient of curries and other dishes and is made in various ways.

Reconstitute 'creamed' coconut which comes in butter-like slabs by soaking 1 tablespoon of creamed coconut in 2 tablespoonsful of water and stirring.

Soak fresh coconut flesh, which has been well chopped, in enough water to cover it, for 3 hours. Then drain the milk into a bowl and put the flesh into a muslin bag and squeeze out the last of the milk.

Or pour ½ pint hot milk over 4 oz desiccated coconut and leave it to stand for ½ hour before straining through a muslin bag.

PECAN NUTS

Native American nut, now imported here around Christmas time. These can be made into pecan nut butter by grinding in an electric blender without additional oil.

Apart from being eaten raw, the nuts are the basic recipe of American pecan pie.

Pecan Pie

Pie case	4 oz chopped pecans
2 tbspn butter	1 tbspn rum
4 oz moist brown sugar	Pinch salt
3 tbspn golden syrup	

Cream together the butter and sugar and beat in the eggs, add the other ingredients and stir well together. Fill the pie case, which should be partly baked, and bake in a moderate oven until a knife put into the filling comes out clean. See also Maple Sauce, page 142.

PINE NUTS or PINE KERNELS

These are the kernels of pine cones and taste a little like almonds. They look like great big grains of fat rice, or very minute almonds! Sometimes called 'pignole' by cooks, they are an ingredient of Pesto (see page 146) and stuffed Vine Leaves (see page 84). Pine nuts can in fact be used in any recipe as a substitute for small amounts of chopped almonds, but are much more expensive than almonds so are not often used this way.

PISTACHIO

Pistachio are very small, but very delicious, rather salty nuts. Add them to home-made pâtés as an optional extra ingredient to give contrast of taste and texture.

Melon Fritters with Pistachio Nuts

Melon	Light batter
Ground ginger	Pistachio nuts
Caster sugar	Lemon peel
Rum or brandy	Frying oil

Peel and slice a melon, removing the seeds. The slices should be about $\frac{1}{2}$ inch thick. Put the pieces in a dish and sprinkle them well with brandy or rum, chopped yellow lemon peel and ground ginger and caster sugar. Leave them to marinate for an hour and then dip each piece in butter (see page 140) and fry in deep fat until golden brown. Remove, and serve dusted with icing sugar and sprinkled with chopped pistachio nuts.

Pistachio Nut Meringue Soufflé

A rather extravagant and complicated sweet, but well worth trying if you like to make this kind of dish for a special occasion.

½ pint cream	4 oz pistachio nuts
Lemon	Whites of 2 eggs
2 oz caster sugar	1 oz butter
Icing sugar	1 tbspn orange flower water, or
1 oz plain flour	a few drops of Cointreau
6 eggs	Vanilla essence

Put together in a deep fireproof dish the cream, caster sugar and the very finely chopped yellow peel of the lemon. Stand the dish in a bain marie (another dish of water) and put it in a warm place, over or at the side of the stove for ½ hour.

Put into a saucepan the flour and butter, heat gently and mix till smooth; add the cream mixture and heat to boiling. Beat up the 6 eggs and add the flavourings and 3 oz of the blanched nuts. Remove the cream mixture from the heat and combine all these ingredients in the pan. Stir the mixture over a low heat until it is a thick batter and then turn it into a well buttered fireproof dish. Cover it with meringue by beating the egg whites until stiff, piping it on as rosettes if you wish the dish to look very special. Dust it over with icing sugar and put it back into the bain marie and bake in a very low oven until the meringue has turned light fawn. Sprinkle the rest of the pistachio nuts over the top, and serve at once.

Pistachio Pilau

½ lb long grain rice	1 pint chicken stock
2 oz pistachio nuts	1 tspn mace
2 oz almonds or pine nuts	Small pieces of left-over chicken
2 oz butter	

Cook the rice in the chicken stock. Blanch and cut up the almonds into slivers and remove shells and inner skins from the pistachios. Use the pine nuts as they are. Cook the nuts together in the melted butter for 5 minutes, stirring so that they do not burn. Add the chicken pieces. Then stir in the rice and heat for a few minutes. Serve piping hot.

SEEDS

In the East toasted seeds are nibbled as we eat peanuts or potato crisps. In the souks of Tunisia little boys heat up seeds over charcoal braziers and sell them in screws of newspaper—a whisky bottle cap being used as a measure.

Chinese food shops sell dried seeds by the bagful, but it is perfectly feasible to save and prepare seeds yourself.

Sunflower, pumpkin, melon or watermelon seeds should all be first boiled for about an hour and a half in a little salted water. Drain them well and cook them in a very slow oven, using the lowest setting possible. Stir them around every 15 minutes until the seeds are crisp. This can take from $\frac{1}{2}$ hour to an hour according to the type. Sprinkle them with salt and eat them while warm and crisp.

WATER CHESTNUTS

These are a common ingredient of Chinese cookery, and they can be bought here in tins. They are very crisp and are excellent added to any Chinese type of vegetable as a garnish. Add the sliced chestnuts for the last 3 minutes of cooking only. Also use them to garnish salads.

Water Chestnut, Bean Sprout and Ham Salad

1 tin or its equivalent in fresh bean sprouts
1 small tin water chestnuts
1 small tin pineapple chunks or lichees
½ green pepper
¼ pint mayonnaise
1 tspn soy sauce
1 tspn curry powder
Slices of best ham
Prawns or shrimps
Lettuce

Drain and dry the bean sprouts, and mix them with the sliced chestnuts, sliced pepper and the pineapple chunks or lichees cut into small pieces. Mix together the mayonnaise, soy and curry powder and pour it over the vegetables, making sure that they are well coated.

Make up individual plates or bowls of lettuce with a heap of the salad mixture in the middle, garnished all round with the ham made into small rolls, and shrimps or prawns. Serve with rye bread or pumpernickel.

Water Chestnuts with Pork

4 oz diced pork	2 tspn soy sauce
2 oz water chestnuts	1 tspn cornflour
2 oz chopped mushrooms	1 tspn sesame oil
1 medium chopped onion	Salt and pepper
1 tin bean sprouts	Olive oil

Cook the pork in the olive oil and season it. Add the vegetables and cook for another 2 or 3 minutes. Mix the soy, cornflour and a little water and simmer with the other ingredients. Just before serving stir in the sesame oil.

Eat this with boiled egg noodles, crispy noodles or rice.

See also Spring rolls (page 61) and Palm Heart Salad (page 71).

SECTION TWELVE

Sauces, Batters Mayonnaise, Dressings, Syrups and Oils

A good cook is known by his sauces, and no aspirant to that reputation could bear to offer only basic brown gravy out of a packet. This section, therefore, contains recipes for quite a few sauces, some of which are the basic sauces, which have widespread uses in cooking. Nevertheless delicatessen do sell almost every sauce, mayonnaise and dressing that you can think of in packets, tins and bottles, and there is really no need at all to make your own, except that good though they may be, ready-made sauces never quite reach the perfection of freshly cooked ones. They are usually much more expensive as well.

There are some exceptions—sauces which have special ingredients, or are specially made and usually themselves ingredients of home-made sauces. Tabasco, Worcestershire, and Soy sauces in particular. Chilli sauce, mushroom ketchup, anchovy sauce and tomato ketchup can all be made at home, but it seems a little pointless when you probably only need a teaspoonful or two at a time to add to other sauces.

Many foods are sold by delicatessen already in sauce; particularly canned goods. These sauces may be very good, but can usually stand a bit of touching up. For instance, anything canned in red wine sauce will be improved by the addition of a little extra wine. In the same way food canned in sauce which does not contain wine may often be vastly improved by the addition of a little (see page 41). As a generalisation, add white wine to fish and chicken, red wine to game and meat.

When stock is required for sauce, of course it is best to make it by simmering bones and vegetables in the traditional way, or by using juices which have come from the cooking food; but stock cubes and powders are an extremely useful substitute. But most of them contain monosodium glutamate and salt and other additives to enhance flavour, so it is almost impossible to get ready-made stock which is not salty. So, when using stock cubes or powder, cut down on the amounts of salt to be added to the dish or sauce. If you are reducing the stock the bulk will be less but the saltiness just more concentrated.

The making of stocks, court bouillons, aspic, etc., is fully covered in any good general cookery book.

Sweet sauces such as maple or corn syrup must be bought ready-made because they cannot be made at home in this country. Other sweet sauces—chocolate sauce, apple sauce, etc., can be bought or made at home as you feel inclined.

All the sauces in this section may be eaten with various dishes. Detailed elsewhere under specific ingredient headings are several 'one job' sauces. Check under 'Sauces' in the Index.

AIOLI (Garlic Mayonnaise)

2 egg yolks
⅓ pint olive oil
Salt and pepper

Lemon juice
2 cloves garlic
½ tspn dried basil or dill

Pound or press the garlic very thoroughly. Put into it the beaten egg yolks with the seasonings, then beating all the time add the oil extremely slowly, drop by drop. If you add the oil too quickly the sauce will curdle.

ANGOSTURA BITTERS

The other vital ingredient in pink gin. It is very aromatic, sharp and strong, and a few drops of it will brighten up meat casseroles.

AVGOLEMNO SALTSA (Egg and Lemon Sauce)

2 tbspn flour
1 oz butter
½ pint stock

2 eggs
Juice of 1 lemon
2 tbspn cold water

Make a roux with the butter and flour. Cook for a few minutes then add the hot stock slowly, stirring it in well. Beat the eggs until they are frothy and add to them the lemon juice and cold water. Beat again thoroughly. Stir in the hot stock very slowly and heat it all again, but do not let it boil or it will curdle.

Make this sauce in a double saucepan if you have one, otherwise use a china basin over a pan of hot water. Eat with vine leaves, aubergines, etc.

BATTER

In Britain, batter is usually made by mixing together plain flour, beaten egg, milk and a little salt, using more or less milk according to the thickness required. But a much better frying batter can be made with the following ingredients:

8 oz plain flour
2 eggs
4 tbspn olive oil

6 tbspn milk
½ tspn salt
1 tbspn Cognac

Separate the eggs, and combine all the ingredients except the whites. Leave the batter for at least half an hour and just before using it, fold in the stiffly beaten egg whites

A light frying batter which comes out very crisp can be made by substituting beer for milk. Combine 2 eggs, 8 oz flour, ½ teaspoonful of salt, and add beer to achieve the required consistency. Adding ½ teaspoonful of baking powder will make the batter lighter still. Add a tablespoonful of rum when making batter for sweet fritters.

All batter is improved by being left in a warm place for half an hour before use.

BÉCHAMEL SAUCE

1 oz plain flour
1 oz butter

½ pint milk
Salt and pepper

Basic white sauce made with a 'roux'. Melt the butter in a saucepan, remove it from the heat and add the flour, blending well. Return it to the heat and cook for a minute or two, stirring all the time. Add the milk gradually, still stirring until it is blended in and smooth. Simmer it very slowly for 10 minutes before serving.

BREAD SAUCE WITH CLOVES (See page 156).

CHILLI SAUCE

4 lb tomatoes	1 tspn black pepper
3 green peppers	1 tspn allspice
3 chillis or more according to taste	1 tspn ground cloves
	1 tspn ginger
2 large onions	1 tspn cinnamon
4 oz moist brown sugar	1 tspn nutmeg
½ pint cider vinegar	1 tspn celery seed
1 tspn salt	½ oz dry mustard

Put all the vegetables through a mincer, and then combine all the ingredients together. Simmer them for about 3 hours, stirring frequently. Add salt and more chopped chillies if the sauce is not strong enough. When cool, put it through a blender and then seal it in small jars.

A hot, piquant sauce to eat with steaks and meat dishes.

HERB BUTTERS (Parsley butter, fennel butter, dill butter, etc.)

Herb butters are excellent with hot vegetables, potatoes, carrots, green peas, beans and white fish. They are made simply by chopping fresh herbs very finely and blending them with butter and salt to taste. Use 1 tablespoonful of chopped herb to 4 tablespoonsful of butter.

HOLLANDAISE SAUCE

2 tbspn fish stock or water	1 dssrtspn lemon juice
1 dssrtspn tarragon vinegar	Salt
2 egg yolks	Cayenne pepper
2 oz butter	

Put the stock, vinegar and egg yolks into a basin and stand this in a saucepan of hot water, or use a double saucepan. Whisk continually until the sauce thickens, then add the butter and stir until it has melted. Season to taste, and then very slowly add the lemon juice. Do not let this sauce boil.

A basic, sharp white sauce.

MAPLE SYRUP

Made from the sap of the maple tree, maple syrup is a sweet liquid, like honey, but runnier and with its own distinctive flavour. It is used straight poured over hot pancakes, waffles, hot bread and biscuits, and really goes with anything which one might eat with honey or golden syrup. It also has many cookery uses.

Once maple syrup has been opened, unlike honey, it will not keep indefinitely.

Ham Steaks cooked in Maple Syrup

Unsmoked ham or gammon 1½ in thick, with rind removed
1 dssrtspn French mustard
Cupful maple syrup
Cloves
Little white wine or cider

Stick a few cloves into the steaks and lay them in a fireproof dish. Mix the syrup with the mustard and a little wine, and pour it over the steaks. Cook uncovered in a low oven, 350 deg. (gas 3/4) for about an hour, basting several times and turning the steaks when they brown. Be sure the liquid does not reduce too much. When the steaks are done, remove them to a serving dish and reduce the gravy if necessary, before pouring it back over the ham. Serve with mashed potato and buttered carrots or parsnips.

Maple Candy

One of the easiest possible ways to make candy is to boil maple syrup very slowly until it reaches 233 deg. F. Then let it cool to 110 deg. without stirring it. Add vanilla essence to taste and beat the mixture until it is light and fluffy and beginning to solidify. Put it in moulds or tins, and when cool, cut it into squares. Store the candy in a container with a tight fitting lid.

Maple Sauce

½ pint maple syrup   2 oz chopped pecans or almonds

Add the nuts to syrup which has been simmering for 5 minutes. Cook for 5 minutes more, cool and use on ice cream, milk puddings, pancakes and waffles.

Maple Syrup Mousse

3 eggs, separated	Pinch salt
1 large carton double cream	Small cupful maple syrup

Heat the maple syrup until it is runny but not boiling. Beat the egg yolks and put them in a double saucepan or in a bowl lodged in the top of a saucepan containing boiling water, beating hard all the time, slowly add the maple syrup and continue cooking without ever letting the mixture settle or boil, until it becomes custard, and will coat a wooden spoon. Put the custard aside to cool right down. When it is cool, beat the egg whites with a pinch of salt until they are really stiff, and whip the cream until it is also very thick. Carefully fold the egg whites and cream into the maple custard, and put it all into a shallow dish in the freezing compartment of the fridge. Freeze the mousse until it is just nicely firm, but not solid like ice cream. Pour a little maple syrup over each serving.

MAYONNAISE

1 egg yolk	Pinch salt and black pepper
1 tspn caster sugar	Olive oil
1 tspn French mustard	
Juice of ½ lemon, or ½ tbspn wine vinegar	

The colder the egg yolks, the easier it is to make mayonnaise, so stand the mixing bowl in another bowl of iced water.

Beat up the egg yolk with the seasonings and sugar. Then, if you are using a hand beater, add the oil drop by drop, beating all the time, until the desired consistency is reached, about that of thick custard. When using a fast mechanical blender, the oil can be added a little more quickly. From time to time add a few drops of lemon juice. If the sauce curdles or does not thicken, it can usually be resurrected by using another egg yolk. Put this second egg yolk in another bowl and beat it, then beating all the time, add the original mixture very slowly.

This produces a basic mayonnaise to which any herb flavouring that you like can be added (see page 151).

MOUSSELINE SAUCE (Green)

1 green pepper
6 anchovy fillets
2 gherkins
1 tspn capers
Handful tarragon and chervil
1 shallot
5 raw egg yolks
Juice of 1 lemon
1 tbspn chopped parsley
1½ oz butter
Salt and pepper

Put the chopped pepper, gherkins, capers, tarragon, chervil, shallot and parsley in a bowl and blend either by pounding, or putting through an electric blender. Add the rest of the ingredients, put them in a double saucepan (or a china bowl over hot water), and whip the contents together until they thicken. Eat with fish, globe artichokes, asparagus.

MUSTARD SAUCE

Thick cream   Dijon mustard

Add one third of Dijon mustard to two thirds very thick cream, and stir them carefully together.

Mustard and Dill Sauce

4 tspn French mustard
1 tspn English mustard
1½ oz caster sugar
2 tbspn wine vinegar
6 tspn olive oil
3 tspn fresh dill or 1 tspn dried dill

Mix the mustards, sugar and vinegar, then slowly beat in the oil until it becomes thick like a mayonnaise. Stir in the chopped dill. This sauce will keep for a few days in a screw-top bottle in the fridge, but the ingredients may settle out, so shake it well before using it.

NEAPOLITAN SAUCE

2 lb chopped tomatoes
1 small tin tomato purée
2 large chopped carrots
2 stalks chopped celery
1 chopped Spanish onion
1 chopped clove garlic
2 tbspn olive oil
Grated rind of ½ lemon
1 tspn chopped basil
Salt and black pepper

Mix the tomatoes, tomato purée, carrots, onion, celery, garlic, lemon rind and basil. Simmer them all for 1½ hours, then press through a sieve, or blend with a liquidiser. Add the salt and pepper to taste, and simmer again until it is thick. Just before serving stir in the olive oil.

Eat with pasta, meat and poultry.

OILS

Cooking oils are extracted from various seeds. They divide into two categories, those which are used to impart their own flavour, and those which are used because they have no flavour of their own. The 'cooking oils' sold in this country are generally of the second type. These include *Peanut* or *Ground Nut Oil, Poppyseed Oil, Sunflower Oil* and *Corn Oil*.

Olive Oil, on the other hand, has a very definite flavour, and this varies according to where it is grown and which pressing it is. Use first-grade oil for cooking, but try Italian, Spanish, Greek and French olive oil to discover which you like best.

Sesame Seed Oil has a very nutty flavour (in fact ground sesame seeds produce something very like peanut butter) and is used for cooking biscuits, cakes and a marvellous confection called Halva. *Mustard Seed Oil* has a distinct flavour and is used a lot in Indian dishes.

When using a recipe containing olive oil, try and use oil from the country of origin of the recipe, if you know it.

PERIGEUX SAUCE

1 small tin truffle peelings	Salt and pepper
Brandy or Madeira	1 cup thick brown stock
Butter	

Use as a base for this sauce either reduced gravy from a roast, or Sauce Espagnole, thickened slightly with a roux of flour and butter. Cook the truffles for a minute or two in butter then drain them and put them on one side, retaining the juices. Add a tablespoonful of Madeira or brandy, and the stock and simmer together for 2 minutes. Then add the truffles and another tablespoonful of Madeira or brandy and season to taste. Reheat, but do not boil. If the sauce is a little thick, dilute it with the liquor from the truffle tin. Eat with meat, game, etc.

PESTO

2 oz fresh basil or 1 tbspn dried
2 oz pine nuts
2 oz Parmesan cheese
2 oz olive oil
1 clove garlic
Salt

Pound together all the ingredients (except the olive oil) until they are smooth, then add the olive oil drop by drop, blending it in thoroughly until the sauce has the consistency of whipped cream.

Parsley or marjoram can be substituted for the basil, but the flavour will be quite different.

Excellent with spaghetti or minestrone soup, which then becomes 'Pistou' soup.

ROQUEFORT DRESSING

To a ¼ pint of sauce vinaigrette, crumble 2 tablespoonsful of Roquefort cheese. Mix well before serving.

SAUCE ESPAGNOLE

1 onion
1 carrot
2 oz mushrooms
2 oz lean bacon or ham
2 oz butter
2 oz flour
1 pint stock
Bouquet garni
6 peppercorns
1 bay leaf
2 tbspn tomato purée
⅛ pint sherry

Slice the vegetables and chop the ham. Melt the butter and gently fry first the ham and then the vegetables until they are golden. Add the flour slowly and stir in continuing cooking all the time. Add the stock, herbs and spices and stir until everything is boiling. Simmer for ½ hour. Then put in the tomato purée and simmer for another ½ hour. Rub through a sieve or put through a blender, add the sherry and reheat.

This makes a very tasty basic meat sauce.

SAUCE TARTARE

1 hard-boiled egg yolk
½ pint olive oil
1 tbspn wine vinegar
1 raw egg yolk
Salt and pepper

Mustard
1 dssrtspn chopped capers
1 dssrtspn chopped chives
1 tbspn chopped tarragon

Mix the sieved egg yolk with the beaten raw egg yolk. Add the oil drop by drop, beating all the time, then add the vinegar and seasonings. Lastly add the blanched tarragon, and the chives and capers. Eat with fish and shellfish.

SAUCE VINAIGRETTE

3 parts olive oil
1 part wine vinegar
Salt and pepper

Mustard
Pinch of sugar

Mix the seasonings with the vinegar and add the oil drop by drop, whisking all the time.

SESAME SEED SAUCE

2 oz sesame seeds
2 tbspn demarara sugar

2 tbspn soy sauce
2 tbspn wine vinegar

Put the seeds on a fireproof dish or tin and toast them under the grill. When they are cold grind them as small as possible and mix them with the other ingredients in an electric blender until thoroughly amalgamated.

This is an excellent sauce with rice dishes, Chinese dishes, or anything which might be improved by a nutty sweetish sauce.

SKORTHALIA (Garlic Sauce)

Up to 6 cloves garlic
5 medium boiled potatoes or 2 thick slices of stale bread
1 pint olive oil

1 tbspn wine vinegar or lemon juice
Salt to taste

Press or pound the garlic well. Put the potatoes or bread through a mincer and mix with the garlic. Put the lot through a blender or pound it until it is quite smooth. Add the olive oil and wine vinegar or lemon juice drop by drop as for a mayonnaise, beating continually, and when blended, stir in a small cup of cold water.

6 cloves of garlic makes a powerful sauce, 2 cloves is enough for most English palates!

Eat with aubergines, courgettes, stuffed vine leaves, steak.

SOY SAUCE

A common ingredient of Chinese cooking which also has its uses for other dishes. It will darken gravies and sauces and add flavour to them, and a dash of soy adds flavour to risottos, egg dishes and stews. It is not at all vinegary or sharp, rather more bland and slightly sweet.

Soy and Garlic Sauce

Add 2 cloves of crushed garlic to ¼ pint soy sauce and simmer for 2 minutes.

Soy and Ginger Sauce

Add 2 teaspoonsful chopped ginger to ¼ pint soy, simmer for 2 minutes and strain before use.

SPANISH TOMATO SAUCE

1 chopped green pepper
1 chopped red pepper
1 chopped chilli
1 chopped onion
1 chopped clove garlic
2 tbspn olive oil
1 tbspn chopped parsley
1 tin tomatoes
1 wineglass sweet sherry, white wine or Madeira
1 tspn salt

Fry the peppers, onion and garlic in the oil. Add the wine, parsley, tomatoes and salt. Cook for about half an hour until the mixture is soft. Good with grills, steaks, pasta.

SWEET AND SOUR SAUCE

2 tbspn vinegar
2 tbspn brown sugar
1 tbspn cornflour
Salt and pepper
¼ pint chicken stock
1 tspn tomato purée

Blend together the vinegar, sugar and cornflour and put them in a saucepan, add the chicken stock and tomato purée and bring to the boil, stirring all the time. Use this for all Chinese sweet and sour recipes.

TABASCO SAUCE

This popular American sauce is made from hot tabasco peppers and a few drops in soups, piquant sauces, stews, and meat dishes will hot it up and add peppery flavour.

TAHINA

A Middle-Eastern sauce which can be bought ready-made in delicatessen specialising in Middle-Eastern foods, or it can be made at home. Its basic ingredient is sesame seeds, and these are available, but are expensive. The result is not unlike peanut butter in texture, but with a much more subtle taste.

5 oz sesame seeds	Juice of 2 lemons
Olive oil	1 tspn salt
¼ pint water	Pinch cayenne
2 cloves garlic	

Put all the ingredients (except the olive oil) through an electric blender until smooth. Add a little more water if the mixture is too doughy, and just before use, stir in a little olive oil.

TOMATO DRESSING

½ lb tomatoes	1 tspn finely grated onion
1 tspn lemon juice	Little sugar
2 tbspn olive oil	Salt

Cut the tomatoes into chunks and rub them through a sieve. Mix them thoroughly with all the other ingredients. Use this with rice, salads and hard boiled eggs.

VINEGAR

Malt vinegars, both plain and distilled, have such a strong flavour that they kill the taste of anything else. Wine or cider vinegars, although more expensive, are much better, particularly for any kind of salad dressing, mayonnaise and for mint sauce.

Herb-flavoured vinegars are excellent for making salad dressings.

WINE SAUCE FOR DESSERTS

2 or 3 tbspn cherry brandy made up to ¼ pint with water	4 oz caster sugar
	2 eggs
1 tspn cornflour or potato flour	1 tbspn lemon juice

Dissolve the flour in the liquid, add sugar and heat to boiling point. Stand the saucepan over another saucepan containing boiling water, and add the beaten eggs slowly, stirring all the time, and making sure the mixture does not boil or it will curdle.

Serve this sauce hot or cold. It can be made with sweet red wine or Kirsch if cherry brandy is not available.

YOGHURT SALAD DRESSING

1 carton natural yoghurt	Black pepper
2 tspn Dijon mustard	1 tbspn olive oil
1 dssrtspn caster sugar	Dill, or fennel seeds, or tarragon,
Salt	or fresh herbs, or cucumber

Mix together the ingredients except the herbs, and correct the seasoning to taste, by adding more sugar or more salt as the case may be. This dressing is excellent as it is, but can be given different flavours by adding the suggested dried herbs, pinch by pinch, until the flavour is apparent. Almost any fresh chopped herb can be added to this dressing to give distinctive flavours, and chopped cucumber added to it makes it an excellent relish to eat with cold meats or fish.

In fact this yoghurt mix is a fine base for experimentation in producing piquant herb dressings of all kinds.

SECTION THIRTEEN

Herbs and Seasonings

Delicatessen make a point of selling a far wider variety of herbs and spices than ordinary grocers' shops, and it should be possible to get any flavouring that you need without difficulty. Specialist delicatessen are always characterised by the smell of the most popular spice or herb they sell. Greek food shops, notwithstanding strong cheeses, olives, garlic and retsina, still reek of oregano, the herb which Greeks add to so many dishes. Underlying this is the smell of sesame seed, so popular in the eastern Mediterranean, which is sprinkled liberally all over fresh Greek bread. Indian food shops are pungent with curry spices, and it takes a good nose to sort out one from the other.

Anyone who aspires to interesting cookery and uses all these new ingredients must understand the uses of herbs and spices and be prepared to keep a good supply on hand. Even though some may be a little expensive, one usually only uses a little at a time, and kept in jars and airtight boxes, most herbs and spices do keep well. There is nothing to say that you should not try adding new spices to standard English dishes. Don't be afraid of them. Ground coriander, for instance, helps to liven up leftover lamb and mutton, and you can use up to a teaspoonful per lb of meat. The above-mentioned oregano is an excellent herb to add to all meat stews and casseroles—the Americans already use it a great deal more than we do, and look upon it as a very common herb. Tarragon is excellent with chicken or fish or tomato dishes, and is another herb to be liberal with.

On the other hand, the Hungarians and others use an enormous amount of paprika to season their food, but to my taste they take things too far. This not so hot variety of red pepper adds colour and an over-riding flavour to everything, yet a sprinkle of it here and there can be very pleasant.

ALLSPICE

Sometimes known as pimento or Jamaica pepper, from which it is made. It looks rather like peppercorn, but tastes like a mixture of cloves, juniper, nutmeg and cinnamon. Used in pickles, stews, and curry powder blends.

ANISEED

A strong taste which one either loves or loathes! Used to flavour sweet cakes and creams, it is also an ingredient in many liqueurs. Aniseed-flavoured sugar can be used for cakes, biscuits and rye bread. To release the flavour, crush the seeds in a folded tea towel with a rolling pin.

Aniseed Drop Cakes

½ lb caster sugar or vanilla sugar
3 eggs

½ lb S.R. flour
1½ tbspn crushed aniseed

Beat the eggs and add the sugar, beating until really creamy. Add the flour gradually, and the aniseed, and beat the mixture for another 5 minutes or with an electric beater. Line a baking tray with foil and drop the batter, half a teaspoonful at a time, on the sheet. If the batter is the right consistency the drops will spread to about an inch. Add flour if the mixture is too liquid. Leave the drops to dry at room temperature overnight, then bake them in the oven at 325 deg. (gas 3) for about 10 minutes. They should be just turning colour and puffed up on top.

BASIL

An aromatic herb with a sweet spicy flavour, not too strong. Italians use the leaves to flavour all tomato dishes, salads and soups, and the fresh leaves are one of the main ingredients in 'pesto', a famous Genoese pasta sauce (see page 146). The southern French also use it a lot particularly in 'pistou soup' which is made by adding pesto sauce to minestrone soup.

BAY

Used to flavour meat stews and milk puddings. Crush dried leaves up to extract more flavour from them. Bay can be bought ready ground.

BOUQUET GARNI (or MIXED HERBS)

Mixture of herbs bought dried in packets, for flavouring stews, casseroles, soups, etc.

CAPERS

The bud of the caper bush, pickled in vinegar and used as a seasoning in stews and sauces. Nasturtium seeds are sometimes used as a substitute.

CARAWAY SEEDS

Have the same type of taste and the same uses as aniseed to flavour cakes, cheese, potatoes and meat dishes, particularly pork. German cooks use them a lot especially with cabbage, sauerkraut and turnip.

Caraway Potatoes with Cottage Cheese

2 lb small potatoes	Butter
8 oz cottage cheese	2-3 tbspn milk or cream
Caraway seeds	Salt

Wash the potatoes and halve them. Dip each cut side into the caraway seeds and salt, so that it is well coated. Put the halves on a greased baking dish, seed side up. Brush them with melted butter, and bake them in a moderate oven until soft. Blend the cheese and milk, and serve it as a separate sauce with the potatoes.

CARDAMOM

A very sweet aromatic spice from the ginger family used mainly in Indian and Arab dishes. Each hard pod contains about 6 seeds. For some dishes the whole lot are ground together, but for curry powders, the seeds only are ground or pounded. Cardamom can be bought ground ready for use.

CAYENNE

An extremely hot ground pepper which should be treated with caution. It is made from a type of capsicum. Sprinkle it on top of *'au gratin'* dishes to colour and sharpen them, and use it in devilled dishes.

Devilled Butter

¼ lb butter
½ tspn dry mustard
2 tspn wine vinegar
2 tspn Worcester sauce
¼ tspn salt
Pinch cayenne
2 egg yolks

Work the butter with a fork until it is soft, then beat all the other ingredients into it.

Spread this butter over any cold game or poultry cut into pieces, sprinkle them with browned breadcrumbs, and put them in the oven in a buttered dish for about 15 minutes.

Devilled Muscatels

Muscatel raisins
Fat for frying
Salt
Cayenne pepper
Ground ginger

Put the clean fruit into the boiling-hot fat and fry it until it is crisp on the outside. Drain carefully, shaking off all the fat, then put the muscatels on to paper towels to dry. Season with salt, cayenne pepper and a little ground ginger. These make a most unusual cocktail snack.

CELERY SEED

The seeds of the plant are used to add celery flavour to various dishes. The main advantage of using them is that they can be kept in a pack in the store cupboard, so that fresh celery does not have to be bought each time you want the flavour.

CHERVIL

This herb is like parsley, with less tightly curled leaves and a milder flavour. The French always put some in herb omelettes, and use it as a general flavouring rather as we use parsley.

CHILLI

Can be bought fresh, red or green, or dried and chopped into little pieces, or dried and ground. Chillies are always extremely hot, and should only be used in small quantities. But the taste for them grows, and people in central and southern America become so used to the hotness, that they eat chilli sandwiches and never shed a tear. The powder loses some of its strength over a period of time, so buy it in small quantities. Be careful to wash your hands after cutting fresh chillis, otherwise you may transfer juice to your face and eyes, and they will sting quite badly.

Dry fresh chillies and chop and store them for future use. Lay the chillies on a piece of baking foil on a radiator and leave them until they are completely dry. Pack them in an airtight jar, or grind them down in a mill and keep the powder in an airtight box.

The main use of chilli is in chilli con carne (see page 121) and other very hot dishes, literally to provide the fire. However, small amounts of fresh chillies or chilli powder can be used to add 'bite' to sauces, mixed vegetable dishes or casserole dishes, without necessarily making them 'hot'.

Chillies preserved in Sherry

Put the chillies into clean jars and cover them with dry sherry. This will preserve them indefinitely, and either the peppers or the sherry are used as flavouring.

Stuffed Chillies

To each 6 fresh chillies
¼ lb grated Parmesan or other hard cheese
1 tspn dry mustard or 2 tspn Dijon mustard
1 oz butter
1 tspn caster sugar
6 cashew nuts

Blanch the chillies in boiling salted water for five minutes, then split them lengthwise and carefully remove all the seeds. Make a paste of all the other ingredients without the cashews. Chop half the nuts and add these to the smooth paste. Fill the chilli halves with this paste and decorate with half a cashew nut.

This makes a very hot savoury cocktail snack, not for the tender palate!

CINNAMON

The best quality cinnamon is sold in sticks, the powdered variety being inferior because it may not be so pure. Cinnamon is sometimes used in meat, game and vegetable dishes, but more often in cakes and puddings.

Cinnamon Sugar

½ lb light brown moist sugar   2 oz cinnamon powder

Mix the two well together and store in a screw-topped jar. Use for flavouring apples, for sprinkling on yoghurt and for making cinnamon toast.

Cinnamon Toast

Sliced white bread
2 oz softened butter
4 oz light brown moist sugar
2 level tspn cinnamon
Rum
Apple purée (optional)

Remove the crusts from the bread. Make a mixture of the sugar, butter and cinnamon and spread it thickly on the bread. Lay the slices on a greased baking sheet or shallow buttered fireproof dish and sprinkle with a little rum. Cook in a hot oven for five minutes. Then remove and brown the tops under a grill for a few moments and serve at once with hot apple sauce or apple purée.

CITRUS LEAVES

Lemon or lime leaves are added to curries to give extra flavour.

CLOVES

Apart from the traditional English way of using cloves to flavour apple dishes, the continentals use them in spiced cakes, beef stews and in sweet sour sauces with game.

Bread Sauce with Cloves

When making bread sauce to eat with poultry and game, put a halved onion with several cloves stuck into it in the sauce while it is cooking, and remove it before serving.

Cloves stuck in Baked Ham

After the ham has been boiled and the skin removed, slash the fat into squares and stud each square with a clove. Baste it with a mixture of 1 tablespoonful of honey and two tablespoonsful of cider.

CORIANDER

This is a basic ingredient of curries. The seeds can be bought whole, or ready ground. In the Far East they are crushed with garlic to flavour meat, and used in soups. The slightly orange flavour of coriander is not sufficiently appreciated by Europeans, although in the past, sweets were made of it. A little coriander improves roast lamb, pork, fish, salads and pickles.

CUMIN

The seeds are rather acrid and spicy. Use them for the same dishes as coriander. Some liqueurs and continental cheeses are cumin flavoured.

CURRY

Curry powder is a combination of spices, dried and ground. Ready-prepared curry powder is made up of about 18 spices, but you can easily make up a curry to your taste by combining varying amounts, from just a pinch of one spice to a spoonful of another, and using from between five to fifty ingredients. Many of the ready-prepared curries are just hot and strong, so it is well worth the trouble of mixing your own ingredients to obtain subtle flavours, or buying from specialist Indian shops which sell loose curry powder they themselves make up. Add a little curry powder to brighten up dull left-overs, and of course use it in mulligatawny soup.

Curry Paste

1 dssrtspn ground nutmeg
1 tspn ground mace
½ tspn ground cloves
1 tspn cardamom powder
2 tspn ground coriander
½ tspn caraway
¼ tspn cayenne pepper
1½ tspn paprika
2 tbspn anchovy paste or
3 tbspn anchovy sauce
2 tspn vinegar

Mix all the dry ingredients thoroughly first, then add the anchovy paste or sauce and the vinegar. Stir carefully. This paste keeps extremely well in a small airtight jar.

Curry Powder (medium-hot)

1 oz ground coriander	1 tspn ground ginger
1 tbspn ground cumin	½ tbspn dry mustard
2 tspn garlic powder	½ tspn ground allspice
2 tspn ground turmeric	1 tbspn ground black pepper
½ tspn chilli powder	1 tbspn salt

Mix all the ingredients well together and keep them in an airtight tin or jar. These quantities make about 3 oz of curry powder, and as all the ingredients are ready-ground or prepared, it does not take very long to make.

Curry Powder (mild)

4 oz coriander seeds	2 peppercorns
4 oz cumin seeds	1 cardamom pod
4 oz ground turmeric	½ oz mustard seed
3 oz dried root ginger	1 dried red chilli

Grind the coriander, cumin, cardamoms, mustard seeds and peppercorns, chop the chilli and ginger as finely as possible, and mix these and the other ingredients thoroughly together. This curry is best made up as needed.

DILL

The same type of herb as caraway and fennel, although each has its own distinctive flavour. It is used as a flavouring for pickles, soups and salads in central Europe and in Russia.

FENNEL SEED

Fennel is like dill and caraway. Italians use it to flavour sausages, stuffings and dried figs. A few seeds sprinkled on to a salad give it an interesting flavour and are supposed to be slimming.

FENUGREEK

The seeds taste bland and sweet, a bit like maple syrup. They are used in curry powders, also sweets and chutney. Fenugreek seeds are small and oblong.

FIVE SPICE POWDER

This is a common ingredient of Chinese dishes and is obtainable at many delicatessen.

GARAM MASALA

An Indian condiment made from the ground seeds of cardamom, cinnamon, cloves, mace and nutmeg. It is usually added to Indian dishes just before cooking is finished.

GARLIC

Much used on the continent, but is uncommon in British food. If it is crushed so finely that it cannot be seen, professed garlic-haters usually enjoy the flavours it produces. It is an ingredient of many recipes in this book. The big white bulbs, consisting of several cloves, are commonly on sale in greengrocers', and delicatessen sell garlic salt, powder or flakes which can be used in cooking for exactly the same flavouring purposes. For those who do like garlic and are not afraid to try it in massive doses, garlic sauce (see page 147), made from fresh garlic, is quite an experience, and so is garlic soup.

Garlic Soup

12 cloves garlic	Sprig sage
2 pints water	Salt and pepper
1 tbspn olive oil	White bread
Sprig thyme	Grated cheese

Crush the garlic and put all the ingredients except the bread and cheese in a pan and boil them for 20 minutes. Strain the liquid through a fine strainer and pour it into a casserole containing about a dozen small slices of bread sprinkled with grated cheese. Add the olive oil and cook in a moderate oven until the bread has swelled and the cheese is bubbling.

GINGER

Ginger is the root stock of a tropical plant grown in the Far East, and it can be bought here in various forms. Powdered ginger is ochre in colour and used as a hot flavouring for bread, puddings, cakes and sprinkled on melon, etc. 'Grey ginger' is sold as fresh root ginger, but in fact is far from fresh although it still has its skin. 'White ginger' is marketed as dried root ginger. These roots have a strong smell and are sold in tubercles between 1 and 4 inches long. 'Grey ginger' is very hard and fibrous, and it takes a sharp knife to cut it in slices, and however much it is cooked, remains rather tough. White ginger cannot be cut, but must be bruised with a hammer before use. They are both excellent for flavouring pickles and curries, but remove the bits before serving, otherwise you will spend an awful lot of time chewing and getting nowhere. In the Far East this ginger is sold when it is young and tender and is sliced or well pounded and smashed before being used.

Ginger juice is best prepared from young ginger, but can be made from the old roots of grey ginger that have been well broken up and soaked for a while in warm water.

The 'green ginger' required by many Eastern recipes can be bought in small tins.

HORSERADISH

It is better to buy this just grated rather than made into sauce as it can then be used as an ingredient of other sauces, etc. Sprinkle a little into mixed salads and add a teaspoonful to a bowl of cole slaw.

JUNIPER

The berries are the main flavouring ingredient of gin. Use a few crushed berries in pâtés and sauerkraut, some stuffings, and with salt pork and particularly in marinades.

MACE

Mace is the dried shell of nutmeg and tastes somewhere between nutmeg and cinnamon. Use it for aromatic flavouring, particularly in stuffings, pâtés and minced spiced meat loaf. It is sometimes used in cakes and biscuits and is sold either in blades, or powdered.

MARJORAM

An aromatic herb used for stews, soups, stuffings and sausages. It is rather like oregano and basil and can be used as a substitute for either.

MINT

Dried mint bought from grocers' and delicatessen never has quite the same flavour as fresh mint from greengrocers' or gardens, but in winter makes a good substitute. Use it with all lamb dishes and new young vegetables.

MONOSODIUM GLUTAMATE

An additive which, like salt, brings out the taste of food. It is a common ingredient of Chinese recipes, which need a sharpening of flavour, and can be used to enhance many flavours. The writer feels that properly cooked food should *never* need this chemical additive to make it taste good.

MUSTARD

Many varieties of continental mustards are obtainable these days, none of them being so simply hot and strong as the English type. Buy small pots of good French, Dijon, Bordeaux, German, etc., etc., which are all rather aromatic, and find out which suits your taste with different dishes. Continental mustards are best for adding to mayonnaise.

In Far Eastern cookery *mustard seed* is used a lot, and is dry-fried before being ground down for curry powder, or else chopped and added directly to the dish.

NUTMEG

Ground nutmeg loses its flavour very quickly indeed, so buy the whole seeds and grate them as needed. Italians put it in most spiced meat dishes and particularly in everything containing spinach. Sprinkle a little on milk puddings, as well as on savoury and cheese dishes.

OREGANO

This is like marjoram, but is rather stronger and very aromatic, and has a more distinctive flavour. Use it in tomato dishes, with lamb or fish, and add a little to stews, risottos, soups, etc. It is very popular in Greece.

PAPRIKA

Paprika is made by powdering dried, sweet red pepper. It is essential in Hungarian goulash and can be added to many dishes to provide red colouring without too much peppery heat. Goulash is quite simply a stew of beef, onion and tomato with a tablespoonful or more of paprika added according to taste. It is improved by being moistened with red wine rather than water.

PARSLEY

Use fresh or dried parsley in sauces, salads, and as garnish.

PEPPER

Use freshly ground pepper as it loses its flavour very quickly. Black peppercorns are simply unripe white ones with the spicy outer husks still on, which makes them very aromatic.

PIMENTO

Ground pimento is made from a type of capsicum. It is usually darker and browner than paprika, but use it in the same way.

POPPY SEEDS

The seeds of the white poppy have been used since 1500 B.C., and still are, for sprinkling on breads and cakes. They give a slightly aromatic sweet flavour.

ROSEMARY

Dried rosemary is rather spiky and many cooks prefer to remove it from the dish before serving. It is a very pleasant aromatic herb, particularly good with veal and fish.

SAFFRON

Saffron is the dried pistils of the autumn crocus, and as there are only two or three in each plant and it takes seventy-five thousand to make 1 oz, it is as expensive as gold. It is best bought as little red threads, for the powder often has additives. Rice cooked in water with a little saffron in it turns a marvellous yellow colour and has an unusual flavour. Crush the saffron before use.

SAGE

Dried sage is never so nice as fresh and has a rather musty taste. In Britain sausages and poultry stuffings are full of it, overpowering everything else, but a little fresh sage goes particularly well with veal. It is often used to flavour wine vinegars.

SEA SALT

This is pure salt made in saltings mostly in France and Spain. It is rather coarse and does not run nearly so freely as ordinary salt, having no additives. The flavour is far better than that of ordinary table salt, but it has to be served in a salt mill.

SESAME SEEDS

These seeds have a nutty spicy taste and are used in cakes, biscuits, sweets and bread in the Near East. They are ground down to make tahina (see page 149), are excellent mixed with ground chick peas to make hummous (see page 118), or mixed with breadcrumbs and spread on hamburgers before frying or grilling. Dip chicken pieces in egg and then in a mixture of breadcrumbs and sesame seeds before frying it in the usual way.

Add a couple of ounces of sesame seeds to any sweet biscuit

mix and sprinkle sesame seeds on home-made bread before cooking.

Sesame Oil is not used as a cooking oil, but as a flavouring in Chinese food.

Sesame Biscuits

4 oz granulated sugar
4 oz butter
½ tspn baking powder

8 oz plain flour
Sesame seeds
2 eggs

Cream the butter and sugar until soft, and beat in an egg. Mix the flour and baking powder and stir it in. Make the dough into a ball and put it on a floured board and knead it lightly for a few minutes. Then make it into little golf balls and flatten them. Separate the other egg and brush the yolk, lightly beaten with a fork, over the uncooked biscuits. Spread a layer of sesame seeds on a clean surface and press the egged side of each biscuit into them so that it is well coated. Bake the biscuits on a baking sheet at about 350 deg. (gas 4) until golden.

STAR ANISE

The other name for this is Chinese anise and it is used to flavour Chinese dishes.

TAMARIND

This comes from the pod of the tamarind tree. Soak a small lump of it in a little hot water for about 10 minutes, and strain the liquid over a curry a few minutes before it is ready to serve. It has rather the same use as lime or lemon juice and 'cools' a very hot curry.

TARRAGON

French tarragon has a far better flavour than the Russian variety. It is excellent with chicken dishes, but don't use too much as the aromatic flavour is quite strong. It is particularly good in consommé and aspic jelly. A sprig of fresh tarragon placed in a bottle of wine vinegar until the bottle is finished, makes the best mayonnaise vinegar of all.

THYME

Thyme is always one of the ingredients in a bouquet garni. Use it to flavour stuffings, stews and meat dishes. It is aromatic and sweet.

TURMERIC

Is a yellow root rather like ginger. It is the ingredient which makes curry powders and piccalilli bright yellow. It can mask other more subtle flavourings, so do not use too much of it in any dish.

VANILLA

A sweet flavouring for cakes and desserts can be bought in essence form or in its natural form as vanilla pods. Essence should be added to dishes only when they are cooling, otherwise a lot of the flavour will evaporate off with its alcohol carrier. Steep pieces of vanilla in brandy and use the flavoured brandy as seasoning. Keep a large jar full of sugar containing a vanilla pod tightly closed and the sugar will absorb the flavour sufficiently to be very useful in cakes, custards, etc. Just top up the sugar as you use it, and occasionally put in a new pod.

ACKNOWLEDGEMENTS

I have often been asked if I have personally tested every single recipe in my books. To be truthful, the answer is 'No'. Had I done so I should be long dead of over-indulgence. No cookery writer can claim personally to have made and eaten every single one of their recipes, and if they do I don't believe them! Actually over the years I have cooked most of the recipes herein. If I have not tried them myself I have used people whose tastes I trust as guinea pigs; or have persuaded them to cook the food, especially if it happens to be something I don't like! One builds up a repertoire of recipes and cooking knowledge from the work and writings of other cooks ancient and modern, with adaptions to one's own skill, tastes, and pocket. So I wish to acknowledge with many thanks the help of these three categories of people; the guinea pigs (family and friends), the good cooks I know, and other writers about cookery whose works are a source of culinary inspiration!

I must particularly thank Ginette Leach who comes into both of the first two categories, and who helps with research and typing. Also Dennis Johnstone of 'The Delicatessen', Walmer, who gave me professional advice from his side of the food business. Charlie West of Mounts Greengrocers, Deal, who stocks and sells the fruit and vegetables mentioned herein, for his help and permission to photograph his displays. And Justin de Blanc, in whose mouth-watering shop many of the photographs were taken.

INDEX

Aioli, 139
Alcohol, 15, 140
  in soup, 15
Allspice, 151
Almonds, 131
  candied, 132
  in Chinese Gooseberry Salad, 88
  in halva, 131
  fillet of sole with, 132
  in maple sauce, 142
  in pistachio pilau, 135
  in sweet spiced pulau, 111
  and trout with cream, 36
Anchovy,
  in artichokes, stuffed, 53
  with herring fillets, 28
  ketchup, 157
  in mousseline sauce, 144
  with mussels, 29
  with rabbit and olives, 69
  in Russian salad, 24
Angostura Bitters, 139
Aniseed, 152
  dropcakes, 152
Apple,
  and lime sambal, 90
  purée with cinnamon toast, 156
  and sweet potato pie, 79
  and yoghurt breakfast, 129
Arles sausage, 48
Artichoke, 51
  hearts with ham and cheese sauce, 52
  marinated, 54
  salad, 52
  and shrimp salad, 54
  soup, 18
  stuffed, 53
  stuffed with anchovy, 53
Asparagus soup, 18

Atta flour, 99
  chapattis, 99
Aubergines, 11, 54
  agrodolce, 55
  curried, 56
  fried, 57
  fries, 55
  Imam Bayaldi, 57
  in Moussaka, 55, 58
  and pepper salad, 55
  purée, 56
  in ratatouille, 66
  raw salad, 59
  salad, 56
  stuffed, 59
    with cottage cheese, 59
    with egg, 59
    Indian style, 59
    with left-over lamb, 59
    with sausage meat and mushrooms, 59
Augsburgers, 47
Avgolemno saltsa, 139
Avocado Pears, 11, 85
  baked with crab meat, 86
  citrus dressing for, 86
  rum and lime dressing for, 87
  soup, 86
  vinaigrette dressing for, 87
Ayrshire Cream Cheese, 98
  in soup, 16

Bacon,
  hock and sauerkraut, 74
  with lentils, 120
  with red beans, 122
  in soup, 119
Bahmi, see Okra, 67
Baked potato with pâté, 49

INDEX

Bamboo shoots, 60
  chicken with, 60
  stir meat slices with, 60
Basil, 18, 152
Batter, 140
  on aubergines, 55
    calamares, 31
    celeriac, 62
    courgettes, 65
    salisfy, 74
    sweet corn, 78
Bauernschinken, 47
Bay, 152
Bayonne Ham, 47
Beans,
  with bacon, 122
  in chilli con carne, 121
  to cook, 121
  red, 121
  soup, 20
Bean Sprouts, 61
  with cuttlefish, 32
  in spring rolls, 61
  in waterchestnut salad, 62, 71
Béchamel sauce, 140
Beef,
  aubergines stuffed with, 59
  Bolognese sauce, 115
  bourguinonne, 38
  in cannelloni, 113
  in chilli con carne, 121
  goulash, 39, 162
  peppers stuffed with, 73
  stew with olives, 68
  tamale pie, 102
  vine leaves stuffed with, 84
Beetroot, 18
Bel Paese, 124
Bierwurst, 48
Birds Nest Soup, 18
Biscuits,
  buttermilk, 123
  oatcakes, 98
  poppadums, 98
  sesame, 164
Bismark Herring, 26
Bisques, 18
Blini, 101

Boiling Sausage, 18, 47
  in cassoulet, 38
Boletus, 66
Bolognese sauce, 115
Bombay Duck, 22
Bortsch, 18
Bouillabaisse, 19
Bouquet Garni, 153
Brandy, 140
Braunschweiger, 48
Brazil Nuts, 132
  roasted, 132
Bread, 98
  black, 98
  corn and buttermilk, 123
  cornbread, 101
  crispbread, 98
  Finnish, 106
  hominy, 103
  linsamerbrot, 98
  oatcakes, 98
  poppadums, 98
  pumpernickel, 98, 137
  rye, 106, 137
  sauce with cloves, 156
  spoonbread, 103
  Swedish, 98
  volkornbrot, 98
Brie, 125
  in pancakes, 126
Buckwheat, 100
  blini, 100
  cakes, 100
  creamcakes, 101
Bummaloo Fish, 22
Butter,
  devilled, 154
  dill, 141
  fennel, 141
  herb, 141
  parsley, 141
Buttermilk, 123
  biscuits, 123
  cold soup, 124
  cornbread, 123
  drink, 124

Cabanos, 48

INDEX

Cabbage soup, 19
Cakes,
  aniseed drop, 152
  buckwheat, 100
  buckwheat cream, 101
  cornmeal muffins, 102
  potato flour sponge, 105
Calamares, 31
  battered, 31
  in paella, 109
Calvados,
  with pheasant, 43
Camembert, 125, 126
  in pancakes, 126
Candy,
  almond, 132
  maple, 142
  popcorn, 116
Cannelloni, 113
Capers, 153
  with herrings, 29
  in Russian salad, 24
Capsicum, 71
Caraway seeds, 153
  and potatoes with cottage cheese, 153
Cardamom, 153
Cashew nuts, 133
  à la diable, 133
  butter, 133
  with Chinese gooseberry salad, 88
  in stuffed chillies, 155
Cassoulet, 38
Cauliflower soup, 19
Caviare, 23
  with blini, 23
  devilled, 23
  in Russian salad, 24
  in soup, 19
Cayenne, 153
  devilled butter, 154
  devilled muscatels, 154
Celeriac, 62
  in butter, 62
  fritters, 62
  in Russian herring salad, 27
  salad, 63

  soup, 63
Celery,
  seed, 154
  soup, 19
Cereals, 98
  popcorn, 116
  rice, 108
Cervelat, 48
Chanterelle, 66
Chapattis, 99
Cheddar Cheese, 125
  in lasagne, 114
Cheese, 123-130
  Ayrshire cream, 98, 125
  Bel Paese, 124
  Brie, 125, 126
  Camembert, 125, 126
  in cheese cake, 125
  cottage, 96, 125, 128
  Coulommier, 125
  cream, 96, 125
  Danish blue, 125, 128
  English cheddar, 114, 125
  Emmenthaler, 124, 126
  Fondue, 126
  Gorgonzola, 128
  grated in soup, 15
  Gruyère, 124, 126, 128
  and herb croûtons, 16
  Jarlsberg, 124
  Mozzarella, 114, 124, 127
  Parmesan, 110, 114, 124
  Philadelphia, 125
  Quiche Lorraine, 128
  Ricotta, 114, 125, 126
  Roquefort, 124, 128, 146
Cheesecake, 125
Chervil, 154
Chestnuts, water, 136
Chicken,
  à la king, 40
  with bamboo shoots, 60
  in birds nest soup, 18
  cock-a-leekie, 19
  coq au vin (2), 37, 40, 41
  livers in Bolognese sauce, 115
  in okra salad, 67
  in paella, 109

INDEX

Chicken—*cont.*
  in pistachio, pilau, 135
  peppers stuffed with, 73
  in sesame seeds, 163
  soup, 19
  in vine leaves, 83
Chick Peas, 117
  and chorizo, 117
  and egg, 117
  hummus bi'tahina, 118
  salted, 118
  in Spanish tomato sauce, 118
Chicory, 63
  and ham in cheese sauce, 64
  salad, 63
Chilli, 13, 154
  con carne, 121
  Mexican tamale pie, 102
  preserved in sherry, 155
  sauce, 141
  in Spanish tomato sauce, 148
  stuffed, 155
Chinese,
  fried rice, 109
  gooseberries, 87
    chantilly, 87
    green salad, 88
    palm heart & bean sprout salad, 71
Chopped meat sausage, 47
Chorizos, 47, 48
  with chick peas, 117
  in paella, 109
  Spanish meat balls, 48
Chutney
  Hot lime, 93
  mango, 94
  spiced lime, 92
Chowder, 19
  clam, 24
Cinnamon, 156
  sugar, 156
  toast, 156
  dressing, 86
Citrus,
  dressing, 86
  leaves, 156
Clam chowder, 24

Clear soups, 15
  to thicken, 16
Cloves, 156
  bread sauce with, 156
  in ham, 157
Cock-a-leekie, 19
Coconut milk, 133
  in dahl, 119
Cods roe, 36
Cognac,
  in soup, 15
Colache, 75
Consomme, 19
  madrilene, 19
  to thicken, 16
  wild rice cooked in, 111
Cooking sausage, 47
Coq au vin (2), 37, 40, 41
Coriander, 157
Corn,
  meal, 101
    bread, 101
    and buttermilk biscuits, 123
    buttermilk cornbread, 123
    muffins, 102
    Mexican tamale pie, 102
    porridge, 102
    Skillet cornbread, 103
    spoonbread, 103
  oil, 145
  sweet, 77
Cotechino, 47
Cottage cheese, 125
  aubergines stuffed with, 59
  in Quiche Lorraine, 128
  potatoes and caraway with, 153
Coulommier, 125
Courgettes, 64
  agrodolce, 64
  fritters, 65
  mint, 65
  provençale 65
  in ratatouille 66
  salad 66
Crab,
  with artichoke 54
  with avocado pear 86
Cracker meal (see Matzo)

Crayfish 25
  in white wine 25
Cream,
  in soup, 16
  soups, 16
  sour, 128
Cream cheese, 125
  cheese cake, 125
  pancakes, 126
  in soup, 15
Crispbreads, 98
Croûtons, 16
  to make, 16
  in soup, 16
Cumin, 157
  rice, 109
Curry, 157
  Aubergine, 56
  paste, 157
  powder, medium hot, 158
  powder, mild, 158
Custard Apple, 85, 88
Cuttlefish, 30
  in soy and sugar sauce, 32

Dahl, 119
  Chamma, 119
  Moong, 119
  Toor, 119
Danish Blue Cheese, 125, 128
Devilled,
  butter, 154
  caviare, 23
  muscatels, 154
Desserts,
  almond halva, 131
  apple and sweet potato-pie, 79
  cheese cake, 125
  Chinese gooseberries chantilly, 87
  custard apple, 88
  guavas, 88
  halva, 131
  lime meringue pie, 91
  lime and sesame meringue, 90
  mango fool, 95
  and rice pudding, 94
  maple syrup mousse, 143
  melon fritters with pistachio nuts, 134
  pancakes, lingon berries in, 93
  passover pasties, 104
  pecan pie, 134
  persimmon,
    ice cream, 97
    with kirsch, 97
  pistachio nut meringue soufflé, 135
  pulau, sweet, 111
  pumpkin pie, 76
  sweet potato, 78
    and apple pie, 79
    patties, 79
  sweet winter squash, 77
Dill, 158
  butter, 141
  and cucumber salad, 129, 150
  and mustard sauce, 144
  and yoghurt salad, 150
Dolmades, 83, 130
Dressings,
  for avocado pear, 87
  citrus, 86
  rum and lime, 87
  Roquefort, 146
  tomato, 149
  vinaigrette, 87
  yoghurt, 150
Dried mushrooms, 67
Duck, 42
  in orange sauce, 42
  pâté truffled, 81
Dumplings
  in goulash, 39
  matzo, 104
  in soup, 15
  yam, 80

Egg
  aubergine stuffed with, 59
  and chick peas, 117
  and lemon sauce, 139
  piperade, 72
  scotched, 50
  with smoked salmon, 34
  in soups, 15

INDEX

Egg—*cont.*
  truffled omelette, 82
  with vine leaves, 84
Egg plant (see aubergine) 11, 54
Emmenthaler, 124
  in fondue, 126
English Cheddar, 114, 125
  sausages, 47
Espagnole Sauce, 146

Fennel, 158
  butter, 141
Fenugreek, 159
Fettucini, 115
Fish, 22-36
  anchovy, 24
  balls, 34
  bummaloo, 22
  calamares, 30
  caviare, 23
  cuttlefish, 30
  dried, 22
  frozen, 22
  gravlax, 34
  haddock, 22
  herrings, 26
  kipper, 22
  octopus, 30
  roes, 35
    caviare, 23
    tarama, 35
  salted, 22
  seafood casserole, 34
  smoked, 22
  salmon, 34
  sole, 132
  squid, 30
  soups
    bisqués, 18
    bouillabaisse, 19
    chowder, 19
  taramasalata, 35
  trout, 36
  with vine leaves, 83
Five Spice Powder, 159
Flour, 98-107
  atta, 99
  buckwheat, 100
  cornmeal, 101
  hominy, 103
  matzo meal, 104
  potato, 105
  rice, 105
  rye, 106
  soy, 107
Fondue, 126
  truffles with, 80
Frankfurters, 47
French Smoked Sausage, 47
Fried Rice, 109
Frogs Legs, 25
  au gratin, 26
Fruit, 85-97
  avocado pears, 85
  Chinese gooseberries, 87
  custard apples, 85
  granadillas, 95
  guava, 88
  Japanese medlar, 93
  Kiwi fruit, 87
  kumquat, 88
  lichees, 89, 136
  limes, 90, 92, 93
  lingon berries, 93
  loquats, 93
  mango, 85, 94
  nectarines, 95
  papaya, 85
  passion fruit, 85, 95
  paw paw, 96
  persimmon, 96
  pomegranate, 85, 89, 97
  soup, 19
Fritters,
  aubergine, 55
  calamares, 31
  celeriac, 62
  courgettes, 65
  melon with pistachio, 134
  salisfy, 74
  sweet corn, 78
Frogs Legs, 25
  au gratin, 26
Fungi,
  boletus, 66
  chanterelle, 66

INDEX

Fungi—*cont.*
  mushroom, 66
  truffle, 80

Game, 37-40
  devilled, 154
  grouse, 42
  hare, 44
  partridge, 42
  pheasant, 43
  pigeon, 44
  quail, 44
  rabbit, 69
  soup, 20
  venison, 44
Garam Masala, 159
Garlic, 159
  aioli, 139
  mayonnaise, 139
  sauce, 139
  skorthalia, 147
  soup, 159
Gazpacho soup, 20
Ginger, 160
  green, 160
  grey, 160
  powdered, 160
  white, 160
Gnocchi, 15
Goose
  in cassoulet, 38
Gorgonzola, 128,
Goulash, 39, 162
  dumplings for, 39
Granadillas (*see* passion fruit), 95
Gravlax, 34
Green Pepper, 71
  and aubergine salad, 55
  in chilli sauce, 141
  in dahl, 119
  in mousseline sauce, 144
  in paella, 109
  in ratatouille, 66
  in Spanish tomato sauce, 148
  stuffed, 73
  in sweet corn fritters, 78
  in tamale pie, 102
  turkey, 72
  in turkey a la king, 40
  in water chestnut and bean sprout salad, 136
Ground Nut Oil, 145
Grouse, 42
  roast, 42
Gruyère, 124
  in fondue, 126
  in quiche lorraine 128
Guava, 88

Haggis, 39
Halva, 131
Ham, 46
  with artichoke hearts, 52
  Bauernschinken, 47
  Bayonne, 47
  in birds nest soup, 18
  in cannelloni, 113
  with chicory, 64
  in Chinese fried rice, 109
  with Chinese gooseberries, 88
  cloves in, 157
  Kasseler rippenspeer, 46
  Knochenschinken, 47
  Krajana, 46
  Lass schinken, 47
  Nuss schinken, 47
  Parma, 47
  peppers stuffed with, 73
  in risotto, 110
  in Russian salad, 24
  in sauce espagnole, 146
  with sauerkraut, 74
  steaks in maple syrup, 142
  in sweetcorn fritters, 78
  uncooked smoked, 47
  with water chestnuts and bean sprouts, 136
Hare, 44
  jugged, 44
Herbs, 151-165
  aniseed, 152
  basil, 152
  bay, 152
  bouquet garni, 153
  butters, 141
  capers, 153

INDEX

Herbs—*cont.*
 caraway, 153
 celery seed, 154
 chervil, 154
 citrus leaves, 156
 dill, 141, 158
 fennel, 141, 158
 garlic, 159
 horseradish, 160
 marjoram, 161
 mint, 161
 oregano, 162
 parsley, 141, 162
 rosemary, 163
 sage, 163
 in soup, 15
 tarragon, 164
 thyme, 165
Herring, 26
 Bismark, 26
 canapes, 26
 gaffelbiter, 26
 matjes, 26
 marinated fillets, 27
 rollmops, 26
 in Russian salad, 24
 savoury fillets, 28
 Swedish hors d'oeuvres, 28
 Swedish matje salad, 28
Hollandaise Sauce, 141
Hominy Bread, 103
Horseradish, 160
 in coleslaw, 160
Hummus, 117

Imam Bayaldi, 56

Japanese Medlar (*see* loquats), 93
Jarlsberg Cheese, 124
Juniper, 160
 in pâté, 160

Kangaroo Tail Soup, 20
Kasseler Rippenspeer, 46
Kirsch, 97, 150
Kiwi Fruit (*see* Chinese Gooseberries), 87
Knackwurst, 47

Knochenschinken, 47
Kochwurst, 47
Kohlrabi, 66
Krajana, 46
Kumquat, 88
 marmalade, 88
 salad, 89
 whole preserved, 89

Lamb,
 aubergine stuffed with, 59
 in cannelloni, 113
 in cassoulet, 38
 haggis, 39
Landjaeger, 48
Lasagne, 113
Lasschinken, 47
Lemon and Egg Sauce, 139
Lentils, 118
 and bacon, 120
 brown lentil soup, 119
 dahl, 119
 and salt pork, 120
 soups, 20, 119
Lichees, 89
 and water chestnut salad, 136
Limes, 90
 and apple sambal, 90
 avocado pear dressing, 87
 curd, 91
 marmalade, 91
 meringue pie, 91
 in paw paw salad, 96
 pickle, 92
 and sesame meringue, 90
 spiced pickle, 93
Lingon Berry, 93
 in pancakes, 93
Linamerbrot, 98
Liver Pâté, 49, 81
 dip, 49
 duck pâté, 81
Lobster,
 with artichoke, 54
 in paella, 109
 in Russian salad, 24
 in seafood casserole, 34
 supreme soup, 17

INDEX

Loquats, 93
Lyons Sausage, 48

Mace, 160
Mango, 85, 94
  chutney, 94
  fool, 95
  and rice pudding, 94
Maple Syrup, 142
  candy, 142
  ham steaks in, 142
  mousse, 143
  sauce, 142
Marjoram, 161
Marsala, 15
Matjes Herrings, 26
Matzo Meal, 104
  dumplings, 104
  omelette, 104
  passover pasties, 104,
  prawns in, 105
  scampi in, 105
Mayonnaise (see also Sauces), 143
Meat, 37
  balls, 114
Melon,
  fritters with pistachio nuts, 134
  seeds, 136
Mettwurst, 48
Mexican Tamale Pie, 102
Milan Sausage, 48
Minestrone, 20
Mint, 161
Mixed Soup, 17
Monosodium Glutamate, 161
Mortadella, 48
Moussaka, 55, 56
Mousseline Sauce, 144
Mozarella Cheese, 114, 124
  in carroza, 127
  in lasagne, 114
Mulligatawney, 20
Mushrooms, 66
  aubergines with, 59
  dried, 67
  ketchup, 138
  soup, 20
  wild rice consomme, 111

Mussels, 29
  in anchovy sauce, 29
  au gratin, 29
  in paella, 109
  in pizza, 29
  in seafood casserole, 34
Mustard, 161
  Bordeaux, 161
  Dijon, 161
  and dill sauce, 144
  English, 161
  French, 161
  German, 161
  Sauce, 144
  seed, 161
  oil, 145
Mutton,
  in cannelloni, 113
  in cassoulet, 38

Neapolitan Sauce, 144
Nectarines, 95
Noodles, 15
Nurnburgers, 47
Nusschinken, 47
Nutmeg, 161
Nuts, 131-137
  almonds, 88, 131
  to blanch, 131
  Brazil, 132
  cashew, 88, 133
  coconut, 133
  pecan, 133
  pine nuts, 84, 134, 146
  pistachio, 134
  to roast, 131
  water chestnut, 136

Oatcakes, 98
  with buttermilk soup, 124
Octopus, 30
  battered, 31
  in paella, 109
  with pasta, 31
  with rice, 30
Oils, 145
  corn, 145
  ground nut, 145

INDEX

Oils—*cont.*
  mustard seed, 145
  olive, 145
  peanut, 145
  poppyseed, 145
  sesame seed, 145
  sunflower, 145
Okra, 67
  and chicken salad, 67
  sautéed, 68
  in tomato sauce, 67
Olive Oil, 145
Olives, 68
  in beef stew, 68
  black, 68
  green, 68
  to keep, 70
  rabbit sautéed with, 69
Omelettes,
  matzo, 104
  truffled, 82
  with stuffed vine leaves, 83
Onion Soup, 20
Oregano, 162
Oxtail Soup, 20
Oyster, 32
  in batter, 33
  grilled, 32
  soufflé, 33
Oyster Plant, 73

Paella, 22, 109
Palm Hearts, 70
  and bean sprout salad, 71
Papaya (*see* Paw Paw), 85, 96
Paprika, 162
Parma Ham, 47
Parmesan, 110, 114, 124
  meringues, 127
  in risotto, 110
  in soup, 15
Parsley, 162
  butter, 141
Partridge, 42
  with mushrooms, 42
  truffled, 81
  in vine leaves, 83

Passion Fruit, 85, 95
  in creams and jellies, 59
  and paw paw salad, 96
Pasta, 112-116
  cannelloni, 113
  cooking, 112
  egg, 112
  fettucine, 115
  filled, 112
  green, 112
  large, 112
  lasagne, 113
  long, 112
  short, 112
  small, 112
  spaghetti, 114
  spatzen, 115
  in soup, 15
  tagliatelli, 115
  types, 112
Pâté, 37
  baked potatoes with, 49
  duck with truffles, 81
  liver, 81
  liver dip, 49
  quail eggs scotched, 50
Paw Paw, 85
  cheese, 96
  and passion fruit salad, 96
Peanut Oil, 145
Pea Soup, 20
Pecan Nuts, 133
  in maple sauce, 142
  pie, 134
Pepper, 162
  black, 162
  cayenne, 151
  chilli, 154
  green, 55, 71
  paprika, 162
  pimento, 162
  red, 55, 71
  to skin, 73
  white, 162
Perigeux Sauce, 145
Persimmon, 96
  ice cream, 97
  with Kirsch, 97

INDEX

Pesto, 20, 146
  pine nuts in, 146
Pheasant, 43
  with apples, 43
  with Madeira, 43
  roast, 43
Philadelphia Cream Cheese, 125
Pickles,
  hot lime, 92
  mango, 94
  spiced lime, 93
Pigeon,
  roast, 44
Pimento, 151
Pine Nuts or Kernels, 134
  in pesto, 146
  in pistachio pilau, 135
  in vine leaves, 84
Piperade, 72
Pistachio, 134
  with melon fritters, 134
  in meringue soufflé, 135
  in pilau, 135
Pistou, 20, 146
Plockwurst, 48
Polnischewurst, 47
Pomegranate, 85, 97
  juice, 97
  in kumquat salad, 89
Popcorn, 116
  candied, 116
Poppadums, 98
Poppy Seeds, 162
  oil, 145
Pork,
  with bamboo shoots, 60
  with bean sprouts, 62
  in birds nest soup, 18
  in cassoulet, 38
  in Chinese fried rice, 109
  with duck pâté, 81
  with lentils, 120
  in paella, 109
  truffled, 81
  with water chestnuts, 137
Potatoes,
  baked with pâté, 49
  with cottage cheese and caraway, 153
  flour, 105
  soup, 21
  spongecake, 105
  sweet, 78
  in wine sauce, 150
Poultry, 37, 40
  chicken, 40
  devilled, 40
  duck, 42
  goose, 38
  turkey, 40
Prawns,
  with artichoke, 54
  with bean sprouts, 62
  in matzo meal, 105
  in paella, 109
  in seafood casserole, 34
  in water chestnut salad, 136
Preserves,
  kumquat marmalade, 88
  lime curd, 91
  lime marmalade, 91
Pulao,
  sweet spiced, 111
Pulses, 117-112
  chick peas, 117
  dahl, 119
  lentils, 118
  red beans, 121
Pumpernickel, 98, 137
  with smoked salmon, 34
Pumpkin, 75
  pie, 76
  roast, 76
  seeds, 136

Quail, 44
  eggs scotched, 50
  in sherry sauce, 44
Quiche Lorraine, 128

Rabbit,
  with olives, 69
Ratatouille, 66

INDEX

Red Beans, 121
  and bacon, 122
  in chilli con carne, 121
Red Peppers, 71
  and aubergine salad, 55
  in paella, 109
  in piperade, 72
  in ratatouille, 66
  sauce, 71
  in Spanish tomato sauce, 148
Rice, 108-111
  Chinese fried, 109
  cumin, 109
  flour, 105
  paella, 109
  pistachio pilau, 135
  risotto, 110
  saffron, 111
  in soup, 15
  sweet spiced pulau, 111
  types of, 108
  wild rice baked in consomme, 111
Ricotta Cheese, 125
  with lasagne, 114
  in pancakes, 126
Rindfleisch, 47
Risotto, 110
Rollmops, 26
Roquefort, 124, 128
  dressing, 146
Rosemary, 163
Russian Herring Salad, 24
  special salad, 24
Rye, 106, 137
  bread with gravlax, 34
  Finnish bread, 106
  flour, 106

Saffron, 163
  rice, 111
Sage, 163
Salads,
  artichoke, 52
    and shrimp, 54
  aubergine, 56
    and pepper, 55
    raw, 59

  avocado pear, 85
  bean sprout, 62, 71
  celeriac, 63
  cheese and paw paw, 96
  Chinese gooseberry, 88
  courgette, 66
  cucumber, 129
  kumquat, 89
  okra and chicken, 67
  palm heart, 71
  passion fruit and paw paw, 96
  paw paw and cheese, 96
  salisfy, 74
  sauerkraut, 75
  water chestnut, 62
  yoghurt and cucumber, 129
Salami, 48
Salisfy, 73
  boiled, 73
  fritters, 74
  salad, 74
Sauces, 138-150
  aioli, 139
  anchovy, 138
  avgolemno saltsa, 139
  for avocado
    citrus, 86
    rum and lime juice, 87
    vinaigrette, 87
  Béchamel, 52, 140
  bolognese, 115
  bread, 156
  chilli, 138, 141
  dill,
    and mustard, 142
    and yoghurt, 150
  egg and lemon, 139
  espagnole, 146
  garlic
    mayonnaise, 139
    sauce, 139
  hollandaise, 52, 141
  maple, 142
  mayonnaise, 52, 143
  mousseline, 52, 144
  mustard, 52, 144
    and dill, 144

INDEX

Sauces—*cont.*
  mushroom ketchup, 138
  Neapolitan, 144
  pepper, 71
  Perigeux, 145
  pesto, 146
  Roquefort,
    dressing, 146
  sesame seed, 147
  skorthalia, 147
  soy, 138, 148
    and garlic, 148
    and ginger, 148
  Spanish tomato, 148
  stock for, 138
  sweet and sour, 148
  Tabasco, 138, 149
  tahina, 118, 149
  tomato, 138
  tartare, 52, 147
  vinaigrette 52, 147
  wine, 150
  Worcester, 138
  yoghurt, 150
Sauerkraut, 74
  hock with, 74
    salad with, 75
Sausage, 37, 46
  Arles, 48
  Augsburgers, 47
  Bierwurst, 48
  Braunschweiger, 48
  Cabanos, 48
  Cervelat, 48
  Chorizos, 47, 48
  Cotechino, 47
  English, 47
  Frankfurters, 47
  French smoked, 47
  garlic in, 38
  Knackwurst, 47
  Kochwürstel, 47
  Landjaegar, 48
  Liver, 81
  Lyons, 48
  Mettwurst, 48
  Milan, 48
  Mortadella, 48
  Nurnburgers, 47
  Plockwurst, 48
  Polnischewurst, 47
  Rindfleisch, 47
  Salami, 48, 114
  Saveloys, 47
    in soup, 16
  Teewurst, 48
  Toulouse, 47
  Vienna, 47
  Westphalian, 48
Saveloys, 47
Scallops, 33
  in seafood casserole, 34
Scampi,
  in matzo meal, 105
Seafood casserole, 34
Sea Salt, 163
Seeds, 136
  celery, 154
  melon, 136
  mustard, 161
  poppy, 162
  pumpkin, 136
  sesame, 149
  sunflower, 136
  toasted, 136
  watermelon, 136
Sesame, 163
  biscuits, 164
  meringue, with lime, 90
  oil, 145, 164
  sauce, 147
  seeds, 149, 163
Shark Fin Soup, 21
Shellfish,
  clams, 24
  crabs, 86
  crayfish, 25
  lobster, 24
  mussels, 29, 109
  oysters, 32, 33
  prawns, 34, 54, 62, 105, 109, 136
  scallops, 33, 34
  scampi, 105
  shrimps, 54, 62, 109, 136
Sherry,
  in soup, 15

INDEX

Shrimps,
  and artichoke salad, 54
  with bean sprouts, 62
  in Chinese fried rice, 109
  in water chestnut salad, 136
Skorthalia, 147
Slicing Sausage, 48
Smoked Salmon, 34
  canapes, 34
  eggs with, 34
  gravlax, 34
Snails, 35
  in garlic butter, 35
Sole fillet with almonds, 132
Soups, 15-21
  additions to, 18
  artichoke, 18
  asparagus, 17, 18
  avocado, 86
  Ayrshire cream cheese in, 16
  bacon in, 15
  bean, 20
  beetroot, 18
  birds nest, 18
  bisques, 18
  bortsch, 18
  bouillabaisse, 19
  buttermilk, 124
  cabbage, 19
  cauliflower, 19
  celeriac, 63
  celery, 19
  chicken, 19
  chowder, 19
  clam, 24
  clear, 15
  cock-a-leekie, 19
  cognac in, 15
  consomme, 19
    madrilene, 19
  cream in, 16
  cream cheese in, 15
  cream, 16
  croûtons in, 16
  dumplings in, 15
  egg in, 15
  fish, 19
  fruit, 19
  game, 20
  gazpacho, 20
  gnocchi in, 15
  grated cheese in, 15, 16
  ham in, 15
  herbs in, 15
  kangaroo tail, 20
  lentil, 20, 119
  lobster supreme, 17
  marsala in, 15
  minestrone, 20
  mixed, 17
  mulligatawnay, 20
  mushroom, 17, 20
  noodles in, 15
  onion, 20
  oxtail, 20
  pasta in, 15
  pea, 20
  pistou, 20
  potato, 21
  rice in, 15
  sausage in, 18
  sharks fin, 21
  sherry in, 15
  spatzle in, 15
  spices in, 15
  spinach, 21
  stock for, 15
  sweet corn in, 17
  thick soups, 16
  tomato, 21
    casseroled cream of, 18
    corn, 17
  turkey, 21
  turtle, 21
    green, 21
    mock, 21
  vegetable, 21
  vichysoisse, 21
  wine in, 15
Sour Cream, 128
Soy,
  flour, 107
  sauce with garlic, 148
  sauce with ginger, 148
  sauce with venison, 46
Spaghetti, 114

Spaghetti—*cont.*
  with bolognese, 114
Spanish
  meat balls in sherry sauce, 48
  tomato sauce, 148
Spatzen, 39, 115
Spatzle, 39, 115
  in soup, 15
Spices, 151-165
  allspice, 151
  aniseed, 152
  caraway, 152
  cardamom, 153
  cayenne, 153
  chilli, 154
  cinnamon, 156
  cloves, 156
  coriander, 156
  cumin, 157
  curry powder, 157
    hot, 158
    medium, 158
    mild, 158
  fenugreek, 159
  five spice powder, 159
  garam marsala, 159
  ginger, 160
  horseradish, 160
  juniper, 160
  mace, 160
  mustard, 161
    seed, 161
  nutmeg, 161
  paprika, 162
  pepper, 162
  pimento, 151
  poppy seeds, 162
  saffron, 163
  sesame seeds, 163
  star anise, 164
  tamarind, 164
  turmeric, 165
  vanilla, 165
Spinach Soup, 21
Spreading Sausage, 48
Spring Rolls, 61
Squash, 75
  colache, 75

  honey-baked, 76
  pumpkin pie, 76
  roast, 76
  sweet winter, 77
Squid, 30
  in paella, 109
  stuffed, 31
Star Anise, 164
Stock for Soup, 15
Succotash, 77
Sunflower
  oil, 145
  seeds, 136
Sweet Corn, 77
  to cook, 77
  cream style, 78
  with colache, 75
  fritters, 78
  in succotash, 77
  and tomato soup, 17
Sweet and Sour Sauce, 148
Sweet Potato, 78
  and apple pie, 79
  baked, 79
  boiled, 79
  dumplings, 80
  patties, 79
Syrup,
  maple, 142

Tabasco Sauce, 149
Tagliatelle, 115
Tahina Sauce, 118, 149
Tamale Pie, 102
Tamarind, 164
Taramasalata, 35
Tarragon, 164
Tartare, Sauce, 147
Teewurst, 48
Terrines, 49
Thick Soup, 16
Thyme, 165
Toasted Seeds, 136
Tomato,
  corn soup, 17
  dressing, 149
  sauce, 138

INDEX

Tomato—*cont.*
  soup, 21
  Spanish tomato sauce, 148
Toulouse Sausages, 47
Trout,
  with cream and almonds, 36
Truffle, 80
  black, 80
  duck pâté with, 81
  omelette, 82
  partridge with, 81
  Perigeux sauce, 145
  pork, 82
  in Russian salad, 24
  white, 80
Turkey,
  à la king, 40
  with peppers, 72
  soup, 21
Turmeric, 165
Turtle Soup, 21
  green, 21
  mock, 21

Vanilla, 165
Veal,
  aubergine salad, 56
  in cannelloni, 113
  peppers stuffed with, 73
Vegetables, 51-84
  artichokes, 51
  aubergines, 54
  bahmi, 67
  bamboo shoots, 60
  bean sprouts, 61
  celeriac, 62
  celery, 19
  chicory, 63
  colache, 75
  courgettes, 64
  kohl rabi, 66
  okra, 67
  olives, 68
  oyster plant, 73
  palm hearts, 70
  peppers, 71
    green, 71
    red, 71
  pumpkins, 75
  salsify, 73
  sauerkraut, 74
  soup, 21
  squash, 75
  sweet corn, 77
  sweet potatoes, 78
  vine leaves, 82
  yams, 78
  zucchini, 64
Venison, 37
  pasty, 45
  roast haunch, 46
Vichysoisse, 21
Vienna Sausage, 47
Vinaigrette, 87, 147
Vinegar, 149
  cider, 149
  herb, 149
  malt, 149
  tarragon, 46
  wine, 149
Vine Leaves, 82
  with chicken, 83
  dolmades, 83
  eggs with, 84
  with fish, 83
  pine nuts in, 84
  with partridge, 83
  stuffed, in wine, 84
  with yoghurt, 83
Volkornbrot, 98
  with smoked salmon, 34

Water Chestnut, 136
  bean sprout and ham salad, 62, 136
  in palm heart salad, 71
  with pork, 137
  in spring rolls, 61
Watermelon Seeds, 136
Westphalian Sausage, 48
Wild Rice,
  baked in consomme, 111
Wine,
  sauce, 150
  in soups, 15

Yam (*see* sweet potato), 78
   dumplings, 80
Yoghurt, 129
   and apple breakfast, 129
   and cucumber salad, 129
   and dolmades, 129
   dressing, 150
   and shrimp salad, 54

Zucchini (*see* courgettes), 64